FIGHTING FOR MY
DESTINY

HOW I LEARNED TO PRAY
TO GET WHAT I NEED

And How You can Do it Too

MAURINE MCFARLANE

BALBOA.PRESS

A DIVISION OF HAY HOUSE

Balboa Press books may be ordered through booksellers or by contacting:

Balboa Press
A Division of Hay House
1663 Liberty Drive
Bloomington, IN 47403
www.balboapress.com
844-682-1282

Print information available on the last page.

ISBN: 978-1-9822-5191-8 (sc)
ISBN: 978-1-9822-5247-2 (e)

Balboa Press rev. date: 05/08/2021

DEDICATION

This book is dedicated to the reader, especially my children Crystal and Blake, and each generation of children they will represent.

May you know God better and draw closer to him as a result of applying the truth of God's Word expressed in this book.

CONTENTS

ACKNOWLEDGMENTS

A special thanks to those who have lifted this project to God in prayer and have continually given me words of encouragement. To my sisters and brothers in Christ, Janice Blakeney, the late Doris Guyton, James Crew, Angela Sharp, Demetrius Lilley, and so many others.

I am especially appreciative of Dr. Arnold G. Fruchtenbaum from Ariel Ministries for his writing on the doctrine of sin. His writing on this subject matter is the most well done and concise that I have ever read. The clarity in his writing leaves no room for misunderstanding or confusion on the subject. For this reason, and in agreement with his ministry for giving me permission to reference his article, I have chosen not to rewrite his work but to reference his words as written.

To my favorite spiritual teacher and writer, Oswald Chambers, author of *My Utmost for His Highest*. His teaching over the years has led me to a deeper, greater, and more enlightened place in my relationship with God. More important, on this journey with the help of his teaching, I have discovered how amazing and perfectly made I am. Thanks to Discovery House Publishers for allowing me to reference his work as a source.

I would also like to thank Ivory Jeff Clinton and Jennifer E. Thomas for their labor of love, professionalism, excellence in editing this book and making sure this body of work represents me.

On your journey to greatness,

may the road you choose to take lead you to peace, love, and joy,

and may the love and grace of God restore you always.

—Maurine McFarlane

My Prayer for You

May the Lord answer you in the day of trouble!

May the name of the God of Jacob set you securely on high!

May He send you help from the sanctuary and support you from Zion!

May He remember all your meal offerings

And find your burnt offering acceptable!

May He grant you your heart's desire

And fulfill all your plans.

We will sing for joy over your Victory,

And in the name of our God we will set up our banners.

May the Lord fulfill all your petitions.

Now I know that the Lord saves His anointed;

He will answer him from His holy

Heaven

With the saving strength of His right hand.

Some boast in chariots and some in horses.

But we will boast in the name of the Lord, our God.

*They have bowed down and fallen, But we have risen and stood upright
Save, O Lord; May the King answer us in the day We call.*

—Psalm 20:1–9 (AMP)

INTRODUCTION

DEAR BELOVED

When I received the revelation from God to write this book, I had no idea what was about to happen to my life—that all hell was about to break loose; the pain, the disappointments, and the challenges that would question everything I believe in; what I would have to overcome would change my experiences, my faith in God, and who I understand him to be.

This is not surprising when considering all the factors. Breaking new ground in what I once believed was God's role in my life requires new language as well as redefining and realigning long-held relationships, assumptions, and beliefs. I found out there truly cannot be a testimony without being tested. So it makes perfect sense to me now that God would allow me to experience this path on my journey of discovering what it really means to surrender all to him. That is where true faith emerges that leads to the manifestation of what I pray for and believe I received.

Before I go any further, I want to disclose this. Before my experiences that led me into a space and time in my life of desolation, distrust, and downright contempt for God, I was a woman of immeasurable faith in God and everything that entails. God was the first person I thought of in the morning and the last person I thought of before I went to bed. I felt loved by God, chosen, and destined by him to do great things.

My spiritual journey in the beginning of my relationship with God was amazing. The revelation showing what was yet to come was at the time overwhelming but exciting. Exciting in that God would choose to reveal these things to me but even more exciting that he would choose the girl from Jamaica who had been rejected by many, abandoned by her own parents. I was on top of the spiritual world, a servant of God and intercessor, one he chose to reveal the secret things to; you could tell me nothing. I was so confident of everything to the point of being spiritually prideful.

So why did things change? And why did life turn against me and lead me to question everything I believed? I met a man one day at the transportation company I worked for. I had to take one of our bus to replace one that was broken down. The person who came to tow the broken bus was a tall white man who looked like the outdoors type. At first, he appeared to be nasty, so I asked him, "Are you in a bad mood?" "No," he said, then murmured something under his breath. After he connected the bus to the towing truck, he instructed me to sit in the front seat next to him.

His truck was uniquely decorated, making it easy to open a conversation with him. I also noticed a Bible. "A man of God, are you?" "Yes," he said. "I am a believer also, and I read the Bible every day," I replied. "A great way to start the day. I love the Lord," he replied. He continues to say, "The word BIBLE means Basic Instructions before Leaving Earth." Wow, I had never seen it completely that way, but when I thought about it, I realized that is exactly what the Word of God is, basic instructions from the one who created us on how to live our best life on earth.

So why are so many of us living the life that is opposite of what God intended for us? Because we are not following the basic instructions of the Word of God. Many people see the Bible as a moral book, and it is, but it is so much more than that. I now realized the state of being that led me to the space to write this book is because I was not following the basic instruction of God's Word. Fortunately for me, God always gives us an opportunity to do it all over and possibly get it right.

In this book, I will share with you many of my experiences that are my testimonies on my journey to finding God. Discovering the righteousness, I have through him that eventually taught me how to pray to get what I need and how to win the fight of my life, the fight for my destiny. This is not a "how to" book or one by some "lecturer of others." This is a book about asking the right questions and what we sometimes must do to rediscover our way back to God, to rediscover who we are in him, so we can fulfill the purpose and destiny of our lives. In fact, God has profoundly convicted and broken my own heart during this past seven years of writing. Yet this deeper breaking has released the presence of Jesus beyond anything I have ever known.

The initial title of this book was *How to Pray to Get What You Need*, but the further I was in the writing of this book, the more I realized I was not only fighting for my destiny, but I was also fighting for my very existence, and I could not get there until I found Jesus again. As a witness to my own life, I have an obligation to tell the truth as it has been revealed to me. Some of you will be inspired; for others, it will not make any difference. But the one thing my experiences will not do is save you. That is because it is never the sharing of personal experiences that saves a person but the truth of redemption. "It is the Spirit who gives life; the words that I speak to you are spirit and they are life" (John 6:63, ESV). My experiences will no doubt be interested to many, but they will not awaken any real sense of need. This need that we all desperately have can only be satisfied or happen once Jesus Christ is lifted up.

Faith that is based only on experience, I have learned, is not faith. Faith that is based on God's revelation of truth is the only faith there is. My experiences are not what make redemption in my life real; redemption is the reality. However, my experiences are simply the door through by which salvation comes into the conscious level of my life so that I am aware of what has taken place on a much deeper level.

According to Prophet Patrick Kiteley, senior pastor of Shiloh Church in Oakland, California, speaking while visiting the New Covenant Church of Philadelphia, what has happened in our lives had to happen so that what is about to happen can happen. This simply means that before we can fulfill our destiny, God must first work out the old man, which can be a painful process, so the new man can rise and conquer.

Before the messages of this book can be of any use to you, there must first be a sense of need created. *Why? Because many of us profess to be happy without Jesus. But if we could be genuinely happy and moral without him, then the question we must ask ourselves is, why did he come?* He came because this kind of happiness and peace is only superficial. Jesus Christ came to "bring the sword" through every kind of peace that is not based on a personal relationship with himself (Matt. 10:34, ESV).

Crises in our lives are either created by God or allowed by God, but the problem is not whether we have crises; it is what we build our house (believes) on. Without a need created in our lives, there is no revelation from God about what he can do in the situation to bring us through. When sickness and disease attack our bodies, God reveals himself as Jehovah Rapha, our healer. When we are faced with financial needs that we cannot handle ourselves, God is Jehovah Jireh, the Lord who provides. The more knowledge we have about God, the more experiences we will share with him and the more confidence we will have on building our belief on God's Word (the rock).

Matthew 7:24–27 (ESV) states, "Everyone then who hears these words of mine and does them will be like a wise man who built his house on the rock. And the rain fell, and the floods came, and the winds blew and beat on that house, but it did not fall, because it had been founded on the rock. And everyone who hears these words of mine and does not do them will be like a foolish man who built his house on the sand. And the rain fell, and the floods came, and the winds blew and beat against that house, and it fell, and great was the fall of it."

Many of us, including myself, want the Christian life. We want to be faithful followers of Christ without the trials and tribulations. Yet in Galatians 2:20 (ESV), it says, "I have been crucified with Christ; it is no longer I who live, but Christ lives in me." These words mean the breaking and collapse of my independence brought about by my own hands and the surrendering of my life to the supremacy of the Lord Jesus. I must tell you, beloved, it is an extremely hard habit to break. It means breaking the hard outer layer of our individual independence from God and the liberation of ourselves and our nature into oneness with him, not following our own ideas but choosing absolute loyalty to Jesus. This requires a deeper understanding of what I thought salvation meant, not merely deliverance from sin but being completely delivered from myself.

My desire to know more about God came out of my need for someone or something greater than myself, a need in my life I could no longer filled. The truth is, there has never been a time that I could give to myself what I needed, but years of living and dealing with the surfaces of my life in disillusion made me think I could.

What happened to me was simply this: for a long time, I wanted to dictate to God how he should bless me, when he should bless me, even the amount. No wonder I was frustrated. I wanted things my way, and when God did not deliver, I began to question his authenticity. God loves us. His word says, "I came to give you life and to give it more abundantly" (John 10:10, MEV), which means nothing missing and nothing broken.

I believe that to get to that place in our lives where we are walking into the fullness of what God has for us, there are lessons we need to learn. Some of us learned through pain, some through joy. Unfortunately, I learned through pain that we cannot be effective until we have been through some things. I must be honest, beloved. At this point in my life while writing this book, I am still in the struggle to totally let go. After all, I am fighting for my destiny, one I believe God has predestined from the foundation of the earth.

So why is it so difficult for me to get there? If this is God's plan for me, why do I have to fight so hard to reach the place where I can say, "Yes, I have made it. I have accomplished the task." *What can stop my destiny? Why is this happening, and why now?* These are the questions I had to find the answers to, and for me to do that, I had to go back to the beginning and rediscover the one I call God. *Who is he? And why does he deserve my total trust and surrender?*

The humanitarian organization that I cofounded, Lighthouse Covenant International, designed and developed a cognitive behavioral program that was taught in the Philadelphia Prison System called Transform Your Mind. It deals with the core of the dysfunctions of the participants' lives by bringing a new awareness to the issues they confront. *We defined dysfunction: Where there is a lack, there is dysfunction. Where there is dysfunction, there is a lack of knowledge. Where there is a lack of knowledge, there is immaturity. Where there is immaturity, misunderstanding is unavoidable. Where there is misunderstanding, there is death in an individual spiritually.* This spiritual death is the separation from God, and whenever we are separated from God, we live in space of darkness, not able to see things quite as clearly.

This is the purpose of this book: to bring a greater awareness to the dysfunctions of our spiritual life, which will eventually manifest itself in our physical life that keeps us stumbling from reaching our destiny.

How do we change this dysfunction? By means of knowledge. The word "KNOWS" in "knowledge" means to bring understanding. It is not the truth that sets us free; it is the truth that we understand that sets us free. *What does this mean for us?* It will change us, transform us, liberate us, and free us. Many of you will have a problem with the statement "It's not the truth that sets us free." The truth does set us free when it is coupled with understanding of that truth. We hear the truth all the time, yet it does not change our lives. That is because we do not understand how the truth connects to our lives to bring us the desired outcome we seek.

You could be a person who loves God and is part of the church community all your life, hearing the Word of God, yet those very words have not had the impact in your life the way it should. That is because you do not understand how to apply the word you have heard to your everyday life circumstances. I know! That was my story, constantly "frustrating the grace of God" (Gal. 2:21, AMPC). That is why God had to take me step by step to enlighten my understanding of who he is so he would no longer be a theory but a living being in my life. This was the hope of Paul for the Ephesians in 1:17 (ESV), "that the God of our Lord Jesus Christ; the Father of glory may give unto you the spirit of wisdom and revelation in the knowledge of Him." It is the knowledge of him that brings forth the reality in our lives, which is the truth of him.

Writing this book has been the most humbling yet life-changing experience of my life. Just like the Israelites who wandered in the wilderness for forty years for what should have been a few weeks' journey, I stayed too long in my wilderness experiences until I came to the end of myself, which meant I finally submitted all to the ways of God, not trying to attach the outcome to myself. And when I did, it opened for me to lay hold upon the greatest power in the entire world—the power of the Almighty God.

In John 12:24 (ASV), Jesus tells us, "Verily, verily I say unto you, except a corn of wheat fall into the ground and die, it abided alone: but if it dies, it bringeth forth much fruit." Unless we come to that place of death of self, as Oswald Chambers called the "white funeral," the burial of the old life, our life, our corn of wheat, is not productive at all. We must die to our preconceived ideas, the fact that we are a product of our environment and philosophy or traditions. And you too, when you get to the place in your life where you are willing to die to yourself. In this context, you must be willing to choose to deny (or die) to your own wishes and completely surrender, and you are willing to say "God, I don't care what happens to me. I just want this glorious experience with you."

In Ezekiel 37:12, the Lord says, "Behold, O My people, I will open your graves and cause you to come up from your graves and bring you into the land of Israel." When God wants to show us what human nature is like separated from him, he shows it to us in ourselves. Then we will know that there is no person who could be as bad as we are without his grace. Yet this book is not written from despair but in the glorious belief that God is doing something awesome! The more you see him, the stronger you will become. *Like me, this may be the time when all the pieces of your life finally come together. Do you hear God's awesome invitation to you?* God is longing to pour his holy presence and power on your life. He longs to sanctify and transform you into the full imagine of Jesus Christ. However, do not approach this process just to "get blessed." Do it because God is holy, and you love him, and for this reason only, he deserves our full surrender

CHAPTER ONE

WHAT IS PRAYER?

*S*o what is prayer? *Talking with God.* Prayer is the practice of drawing on the grace of God. Prayer is our direct line with heaven. Prayer is a communication process that allows us to talk to God. He wants us to communicate with him like a person-to-person phone call. Prayer is not a normal part of the life of the natural man.

We hear it said all the time that a person's life will suffer if they do not pray, but what I have learned through my own experiences and from reading other people's experiences is that our life does not suffer. What suffers is the life of the Son of God in us, which is only nourished by prayer. We see prayer as means of getting things for ourselves, but the biblical purpose of prayer is that we may get to know God himself. When we become born again from above, the life of the Son of God is born in us, and we can either starve or nourish that life.

Prayer is the way that the life of God in us is nourished. Prayer is a precious gift of time that the awesome creator of the universe longs to have with his children. This is a time when we can look forward to each day as we express our love and thankfulness to our Heavenly Father for his calling and grace. It is also during this special time when we come to our loving spiritual Father to talk about our needs, hopes, fears, and concerns for others.

The Logistics of Prayer

Our thinking about prayer, whether right or wrong, is based on our mental concept of it. Many people question what prayer is because they desire to pray but do not know how. There are many reasons for that. It may surprise you to find that one of the big reasons many people struggle with prayer is because of all the wrong teaching they have received about it. I believe one of the culture failings in the church as well as outside the church is the lack of analytical point of view of the system. To have a successful product, you should take the time to explain it properly.

The same is true of having a successful prayer life. Many of us prefer to ask someone else to pray for us instead of going to God ourselves for the answers we seek. But have we ever considered that if we ask someone to pray for us and that person is not complete in Christ, their prayers accomplish nothing? If that person is complete in Christ, their prayers bring victory all the time.

Prayer is effective only when there is completeness. "Take up the whole armor of God… praying always" (Eph. 6:13,18, ASV). Making claims to the promises and walking into the fullness of God will take much more than speaking it and claiming it. To claim the inheritance promised to us by God is a process that will require change—change from what we once believed; a new level of commitment, diligence, and perseverance; and a renewed knowledge of the one you seek the inheritance from.

Jesus never mentioned unanswered prayer. He had the unlimited certainty of knowing that prayer is always answered. *Can you think of a time when it seemed that God did not answer your prayer?* Jesus said, "Everyone who asks, receives" (Matt. 7:8, CEB). Yet we say, "But…but…" God answers prayer in the best way, not just sometimes but every time. However, the evidence of the answer in the area we want it may not always immediately follow. *Do we expect God to answer prayers?*

In John 16:25–27 (AMP), Jesus Christ makes the case for us that he is praying for us: "These things have I spoken unto you in proverbs; but the time cometh, when I should no more speak unto you in proverbs, but I shall shew you plainly of the father. And that day ye shall ask in my name; and I say unto you, that I will pray the Father for you; for the Father, himself loveth you, because ye have love me, and have believed that I came out from God."

When I finally received this revelation, it changed everything for me. I heard it many times that Jesus is our intercessor, that he intercedes for us, but it never had the same impact on my faith as this verse, and I realized why. This is the revelation! Because I love him, Jesus, and I believe he was sent by God, whatever I ask in his name, he will petition the Father for me. So whatever I ask and do not doubt in my heart will be given to me. I can turn over all my cares to God and not be afraid of the outcome. "Our Father knows the things we have need of before we ask Him" (Matt. 6:8, CEB).

Then why should we ask? I am learning that the point of prayer is not to get answers from God but to have perfect and complete oneness with him. If we pray only because we want answers, we will become irritated, disappointed, and angry with God. I went through this experience with God, and it is not a good place to be in one's relationship with God or one's faith in him. We do receive an answer every time we pray, but it does not always come in the way we expected, and our spiritual irritation shows our refusal to identify ourselves truly with our Lord in prayer.

"I do not say to you that I shall pray the Father for you; for the Father Himself loves you" (John 16:26–27, ASV). *Have we reached such a level of intimacy with God that the only thing that can account for our prayer lives is that it has become one with the prayer life of Jesus Christ? Has our Lord exchanged our life with his vital life?* If so, then "in that day," we will be so closely identified with Jesus that there will be no distinction. To say "Prayer changes things" is not as close to the truth as saying, "Prayer changes me, and then I change things." God has established things so that prayer based on redemption changes the way we look at things. Prayer is not a matter of changing things externally but changing our inner nature.

In Genesis 2:8–15 (CEB), God planted a garden in east of Eden. He put the man he had just made in it. God made all kinds of trees grow from the ground, trees beautiful to look at and good to eat. The tree of life was in the middle of the garden, also the tree of knowledge of good and evil. God took the man and set him down in the Garden of Eden to work the ground and keep it in order. He then commanded the man, "You can eat from any tree in the garden, except from the tree of knowledge of good and evil. Do not eat from it. The moment you eat from that tree, you're dead." Today many of us are still eating from the tree of evil and trying to do good. It is the same tree. It never works; it only leads to spiritual death.

We need to follow Jesus Christ's teaching and eat from the tree of life. There it was, planted in the heart of paradise. It was the centerpiece and crowning glory of the Garden of Eden: the tree of life. God had given it to his people as a source of blessing and eternal life. In fact, God had given Adam and Eve everything they could ever possibly need. They even had the manifested presence of God himself. They could walk and talk with him "in the cool of the day." "And they heard the sound of the Lord God walking in the garden in the cool of the day" (Gen. 3:8, AMP). Notice that it does not say only that the Lord walked in the garden but that "they heard the sound of the Lord walking."

The point is, God was physical, substantially present in the garden. Whatever form the awesome sounds took, Adam and Eve heard it. They "heard" God. But they did more than that. They talked with him and fellowshipped with him. This was God's plan for man. What Adam and Eve experienced was the glory of God. In the presence of God, everything is complete.

This is what God has always wanted and still wants today—to be near his children, to delight in them and for them to delight in him. God longs to be close to us. He wants us to hear him and come running into his loving presence. Yes, God gave Adam and Eve everything they could ever possibly need or want. But he gave them something else too; he gave them a choice. He gave them free will to choose whether they would come to the tree of life to partake in his goodness.

God gives us the same freedom of choice today. We can choose to draw close to him and partake in his goodness, or we can choose not to. The man or woman who discovers who they are in God cannot stray from God's best. Matthew 16:18 (ASV) says, "The Gates of Hell Shall Not Prevail against you," which means sickness cannot touch you; poverty cannot touch you. The glory is the part of God that cannot be destroyed; it is a place where God manifests himself.

When Adam sinned, man fell and came short of the glory of God (Rom. 3:23, CSB), and we became separated from the presence of God. But when the second Adam, Jesus, came to earth and died for us, we went back to the original state of the glory. That is why the gates of hell cannot prevail against us.

"Shall not prevail" is from the Greek word *katischuo*, which itself comes from two Greek words—*kata*, meaning "against" or "upon," and *ischuo*, which means "to be strong" or "to have strength." Put them together and you have *katischuo*, which means to have the strength to go into battle against the foe. Not only that, but it also means to have the strength to have the victory over your foe. It is not only the strength to fight; it is also the strength to win. "Prevail" is a good translation, so is "overcome." It is a military term. It is what an army needs to win the battle.

The Turning Point in Prayer

With all that in mind, how can we avoid the frustration that commonly accompanies our prayers? I believe the answer lies in studying the way Jesus prayed. If we want to know what God is like, we must look at the word and works of Jesus Christ. It is necessary for our salvation that we understand the characteristics of God and manifest them (make them known) to others by what we say and do. *If anyone knows how to pray, it was Jesus.* He knew how God thinks because he is God. "I and the Father are one" (John 10:30, NIV). Jesus demonstrated a pattern throughout his prayer life that all of us can copy. In obedience, he brought his desires in line with his Father's. *When we reach the place where we are willing to do or accept God's will instead of our own, we have reached the turning point in prayer.* Jesus lived that. "For I have come down from heaven not to do my will but to do the will of him who sent me" (John 6:38, NIV).

Sometimes in surrendering to God's will, we also cry out as the father of a sick child did to Jesus. "I do believe; help me overcome my unbelief!" (Mark 9:24, NIV) Like that father, most of us surrender our will to God only after we hit rock bottom, when we have no alternatives and God is the last resort. We grudgingly give up our independence and let him take over. It does not have to be that way. When our condition is not conducive for God's presence, he teaches us how to pray (Luke 11:2–4, AMPC).

Our Lord's Prayer

Our Father, which art in heaven, Hallowed be thy Name.
Thy Kingdom come.
Thy will be done in earth, as it is in heaven.
Give us this day our daily bread. And forgive us our trespasses,
As we forgive them that trespass against us.
And lead us not into temptation But deliver us from evil.
For thine is the kingdom, The power, and the glory, For ever and ever.
Amen.

This understanding is important to every person. *Why?* Because we can no longer afford to stumble through life hoping to find the right road. There is no time for that now. We are not here to develop a spiritual life of our own; we are here to have the full realization of Jesus Christ, for building his body. The reconciliation of the human race according to God's plan means realizing him not only in our lives individually but also in our lives collectively. Jesus Christ sent apostles and teachers for this purpose—that the corporate person of Christ and his church, made up of many members, might be brought in to being and made known.

I believe it is essential that every person should understand the fundamentals of who God is, not just what he does and can do. Our life is a direct reflection of who we listen to. The more experience we have with God through his word or any other means he reveals himself to us, the greater will be our knowledge of him and the stronger our relationship will be with him. Naturally our trust and belief in him will also take root, and if we do not allow the cares of the world to distract and confuse us, we will bear much fruit.

Below is the prayer of Jesus according to John 17 (NKJV):

The Prayer of Jesus

Jesus spoke these words, lifted up His eyes to heaven, and said: "Father, the hour has come. Glorify Your Son, that Your Son also may glorify You, as You have given Him authority over all flesh, that He should[1] give eternal life to as many as You have given Him. And this is eternal life, that they may know You, the only true God, and Jesus Christ whom You have sent. I have glorified You on the earth. I have finished the work which You have given Me to do. And now, O Father, glorify Me together with Yourself, with the glory which I had with You before the world was.

Jesus Prays for His Disciples

"I have manifested Your name to the men whom You have given Me out of the world. They were Yours, You gave them to Me, and they have kept Your word. Now they have known that all things which You have given Me are from You. For I have given to them the words which You have given Me; and they have received them, and have known surely that I came forth from You; and they have believed that You sent Me.

"I pray for them. I do not pray for the world but for those whom You have given Me, for they are Yours. And all Mine are Yours, and Yours are Mine, and I am glorified in them. Now I am no longer in the world, but these are in the world, and I come to You. Holy Father, keep through Your name those whom You have given Me,[2] that they may be one as We are. While I was with them in the world,[3] I kept them in Your name. Those whom You gave Me I have kept;[4] and none of them is lost except the son of perdition, that the scripture might be fulfilled. But

now I come to You, and these things I speak in the world, that they may have My joy fulfilled in themselves. I have given them Your word; and the world has hated them because they are not of the world, just as I am not of the world. I do not pray that You should take them out of the world, but that You should keep them from the evil one. They are not of the world, just as I am not of the world. Sanctify them by Your truth. Your word is truth. As You sent Me into the world, I also have sent them into the world. And for their sakes I sanctify Myself, that they also may be sanctified by the truth.

Jesus Prays for All Believers

"I do not pray for these alone, but also for those who will[5] believe in Me through their word; that they all may be one, as You, Father, are in Me, and I in You; that they also may be one in Us, that the world may believe that You sent Me. And the glory which You gave Me I have given them, that they may be one just as We are one: I in them, and You in Me; that they may be made perfect in one, and that the world may know that You have sent Me, and have loved them as You have loved Me.

"Father, I desire that they also whom You gave Me may be with Me where I am, that they may behold My glory which You have given Me; for You loved Me before the foundation of the world. O righteous Father! The world has not known You, but I have known You; and these have known that You sent Me. And I have declared to them Your name, and will declare it, that the love with which You loved Me may be in them, and I in them."

ENDNOTES

1   In John 17:2, M-Text reads *shall*.

2   In John 17:11, NU-Text and M-Text read *keep them through Your name which You have given Me.*

3   In John 17:12, NU-Text omits *in the world*.

4   In John 17:12, NU-Text reads in *Your name which You gave Me. And I guarded them (or it).*

5   In John 17:20, NU-Text and M-Text omit *will*.

CHAPTER TWO

THE CHARACTER OF GOD

One day we all will have the opportunity to meet God face-to-face and understand more about who he is. In the meantime, to a large degree, it is a mystery. He has revealed enough of his nature to man for us to know that we will never understand all of him. The more I learn about God, the more I realize how little I know.

To get a full understanding of God, we must understand the different dimensions of God. There are two theological dimensions of God—the essential or intrinsic and the declarative dimension of God. The essential or intrinsic refers to the excellence of God's nature, his moral attributes, and his divine character. There is nothing we can do as believers or nonbelievers that can add or subtract from God's character. He is who he is.

The declarative dimension of God refers to God's renown, his reputation, or the esteem in which he is held by moral beings. This deals with God's reputation, and as such, a believer's lifestyle can impact the reputation of God by how we conduct our lives. Many will judge God by what those who say they follow him say and do.

I want to explain a bit more about what I mean when I speak about the character of God. The character of God has much to do with the very nature of God. It is deeper than the will of God, for will flows out of character. So my questions are these: *What is God's character? What does God care about? What is God's passion?* Our sense of God's character, our perception of what God is like is carried or conveyed by our images of God or metaphors for God.

I typically distinguish between concepts of God, which I see as more abstract, and images of God. Images or metaphors are more concrete, more visual. Indeed, I sometimes think of metaphors as linguistic art or verbal art. Some of the biblical metaphors for God or images for God include the following: God is like a king, like a judge, like a shepherd, like a father, and less commonly, like a mother. God is like a lover, like a potter, like a warrior, and so forth.[1]

These images for God matter, to repeat my foundational claim. They matter because they shape how we see the character of God. He is not only personal and dwells within man, but he also exalts above all creation. He is active and present in our world and yet superior, absent, and removed from it. He is transcendent.

God in his perfect balance has made himself active and present in our lives so that we can develop a relationship with him. Though we never completely know and understand him, we can spend a lifetime getting to know him better and growing closer to him.

We can find out God's character through a book that was written many, many years ago. It is the Bible, Old Testament and New Testament. In it, many men and women had real everyday dealings with God and his son, Jesus. The very beginning of the Old Testament talks about the creation of the world and of man (Genesis 1). If you look at verse 26 (ASV), it says, "Then God said, 'Let us make man in our image, after our likeness…'" God not only created the world we live in, but he also created us.

Why did he create us? He created us in his own image after his likeness so he could have a relationship with us. So if you compare this type of relationship with a family relationship, he is our father, and we are his children—sons and daughters. As an earthly father loves his children so very much to provide their worldly needs of food, shelter, and clothing, so does our Heavenly Father desire to look after us as his children. This is the characteristic of God, a loving Heavenly Father who sees and feels what we do.[2]

So who is God, and what do we know of him? To answer these questions, I had to go to the BIBLE (Basic Instructions before Leaving Earth), not just reading it but also studying it and spending a great deal of time in the presence of God. He may be described in terms of attributes. An attribute is an inherent characteristic of a person or being. While we cannot describe God in a comprehensive way, we can learn about him by examining his attributes as revealed in the Bible. It is important not to exalt one attribute over another. When that is done, it presents a caricature of God. It is all the attributes of God taken together that provide an understanding of the nature and person of God.

The first group is known as the *absolute attributes of God*. God is Spirit.[3] Jesus taught, "God is Spirit" (John 4:24, JSV). God has no body, no physical or measurable form. Thus, God is invisible. He became visible in human form in the person of Jesus Christ, but his essence is invisible.

God is changeless. Progress and change may characterize some of his works, but God himself remains unchanged (Heb. 1:12, ASV). He does not change; otherwise, he would not be perfect. Thus, what we know of God can be known with certainty. He is not different from one time to another.

God is all powerful. God's power is unlimited. He can do anything that is not inconsistent with his nature, character, and purpose (Gen. 17:1, 18:14, AMP). The only limitations on God's power are imposed by himself (Gen. 18:25, AMP). "Impossible" is not in God's vocabulary. God creates and sustains all things, yet he never grows weary (Isa. 40:27–31, CEB).

God is all knowing. God possesses all knowledge (Job 38:39; Rom. 11:33–36, CEB). Because God is everywhere at once and the same time, he knows everything simultaneously. God having the power to know the thoughts and motives of every heart is evident from many scripture passages, notably Job 37:16 (ASV), Psalm 147:5 (ASV), and Hebrews 3:13 (ASV).

God is everywhere. God is not confined to any part of the universe but is present in all his power at every point in space and every moment in time (Ps. 139:7–12, ASV). Thus, God does not belong to any one nation or generation. He is the God of all the earth (Gen. 18:25, ASV).

God is eternal. Eternity refers to God's relation to time. Past, present, and future are known equally to him (2 Pet. 3:8; Rev. 1:8, ASV). Time is like a parade that man sees only a segment at a time. But God sees time in its entirety.

The second group of attributes is called *moral attributes*. These refer to God's character, his essential nature. God is holy. The word "holy" comes from the root word that means "to separate." Thus, it refers to God as separated from or exalted above other things (Isa. 6:1–3, ASV). Holiness refers to God's moral excellence. Being holy, God demands holiness in his own children. And what he demands, he supplies. Holiness is God's gift that we receive by faith through his Son, Jesus Christ (Eph. 4:24, ASV).

God is righteous. Righteousness as applied to God refers to his affirmation of what is right as opposed to what is wrong. The righteousness of God refers to his moral laws laid down to guide the conduct of humankind, as in the Ten Commandments. Righteousness also refers to God's administration of justice. He brings punishment upon the disobedient (Gen. 18:25; Deut. 32:4; Rom. 2:6–16, ASV). Finally, God's righteousness is redemptive. In the book of Romans, the righteousness of God refers to God declaring the believer to be in a state of righteousness as though he had never been unrighteous (Rom. 1:16–17, 3:24–26, ASV). This is possible because of the sacrificial death of Jesus on our behalf.

God is love. Love is the essential, self-giving nature of God. God's love for man seeks to awaken a responsive love of man for God. Divine love runs like a golden thread through the entire Bible. Nature is eloquent with the skill, wisdom, and power of God. Only in the Bible, however, do we discover God giving himself and all he possesses to his creatures to win their response and to possess them for himself. God loved and gave; he loved and sought, just as a shepherd seeks his sheep. God loved and suffered, providing his love by giving his all on the cross for the redemption of humanity. God, in his love, wills good for all his creatures (Gen. 1:31; Ps. 145:9; Mark 10:18, ASV).

God is truth. All truth, whether natural, physical, or religious, is grounded in God. Thus, any seemingly inconsistent teaching between natural and physical sciences and God's revelation of himself is more apparent than real. Truth is magnified in an absolute way through God's revelation.

God is wisdom. God's wisdom is revealed in his doing the best thing, in the best way, at the best time, for the best purpose. Some people have knowledge but little wisdom, while the wisest at times have little knowledge. But God is "the only wise God" (1 Tim. 1:17, GNV). In creation, history, human lives, redemption, and Christ, his divine wisdom is revealed. Man, lacking wisdom, can claim God's wisdom simply by asking (1 Kings 3:9; James 1:5, GNV).

The relative attributes of God because they are relative to time and space.

Eternity. The eternity of God is usually understood as related to time. It means that God is not limited or bound by time. With God, there is no succession of events; he is above the temporal limitation. "With Him there is no distinction between the present, past, and future, but all things are equal and always present to him."[4] In Psalm 90:2 (NKJV), his eternity is expressed from everlasting to everlasting—"Thou are God." God's eternity is also related to his name. In Exodus 3:14 (GNV), he informed Moses that his name is "I AM WHO I AM."

Immensity. Immensity is defined as "that perfection of the Divine Being by which He transcends all spatial limitations and yet is present in every point of space with His Whole Being."[5] Unlike human bodies, which are bound and limited to space, God in his immensity is not limited or localized.

Omnipresence. In the next three attributes, the prefix *omni* comes from the Latin word *omnis*, meaning "all." Omnipresence means that God is present everywhere. More specifically, omnipresence may be defined as "God, in the totality of his essence. Without diffusion or expansion, multiplication, or division, penetrates and fills the universe in all its parts."[6] Psalm 139:7–12 (GNV) explains the omnipresence of God. From the highest heavens to the depths of the earth and sea, God is present everywhere. There is no escaping God's presence. This definition militates against the idea that God is in heaven, and only his power is on earth.

Omniscience. The English word "omniscience" comes from the Latin word *omnis*, meaning "all" and *scientia*, meaning "knowledge." Thus, it means that God has all knowledge. He knows all things actual and possible, past, present, and future in one eternal act.[7]

Omnipotence. The term "omnipotence" signifies that God is all powerful. However, it does not suggest that because God is all powerful, he can and does do anything or everything at random. A proper definition states that God is all powerful and able to do whatever he wills. Since his will is limited by his nature, God can do anything that is in harmony with his perfections.[8] God cannot do things that are not in harmony with his nature. He cannot go back on his word (2 Tim. 2:13, GNV), he cannot lie (Heb. 6:18, GNV), and he has no relationship to sin (Hab. 1:13; James 1:13, GNV). The doctrine of God's omnipotence becomes a source of great comfort for the believers (Gen. 18:14; 1 Pet. 1:5, GNV).

There are also relative attributes of God that relate to morality.

Truth. In speaking of God as truth, it is implied that God is all that he as God should be and that his word and revelation are completely reliable. God is the truth in his person. He is perfectly complete and completely perfect as God. He is without peer (Isa. 45:5, NKJV). God is the truth in his revelation. It means that he is completely true in his revelation to mankind (Ps. 110:5; 1 Pet. 1:25; Matt. 5:18, AMP). He is reliable. Unlike a mortal, God cannot lie (Titus 1:2; Heb. 6:18, AMP); he speaks the truth and fulfills everything that he has promised to do (Num. 23:19, AMP).

Mercy. A general definition of mercy is "the goodness or love of God shown to those who are in misery or distress, irrespective of their deserts."[9] It stresses the faithfulness of God despite man's unfaithfulness and therefore emphasizes pity, sympathy, and love. God is true in that he will never abrogate his promises (Rom. 3:3–4, NKJV). In concert with the Father, Jesus proclaimed, "I am the truth" (John 14:6, AMP). His word is reliable; his disciples could trust him. It means he will never renege on a promise he has made, such as in John 3:16 (AMP).

Grace. Grace may be defined as the unmerited or undeserving favor of God to those who are under condemnation. The grace of Christ enabled believers to have a positional standing before God (Rom. 5:2, AMP). Christ brought life instead of death through grace (Rom. 5:17, AMP). The grace of Christ exceeded the sin of Adam (Rom. 5:15, 20, AMP). The grace of Christ dispensed spiritual gifts to all believers (Rom. 12:6; Eph. 4:7, AMP).[10]

Justice. Justice is sometimes taken together with the righteousness of God. The justice of God means that God is entirely correct and just in all his dealings with humanity; moreover, this justice acts in accordance with his law. The justice of God therefore is related to man's sin. Since God's law reflects God's standard, then God is righteous and just when he judges man for his violation of God's revealed law.[11]

God's Supreme Power

When we look at God's creation, we find ourselves confronted with so vast an energy that no limit can be imagined for it. A look at creation and the millions of truths secreted in the wonders of nature and the depths of man's own being provides the clearest indication of the scale of the power of the one who has created it, for the rich and complex order of being admits of no other explanation. There is no word to express the dimensions of his power. That unique essence has much power that whenever he wills a thing to come into existence, it suffices for the command.

In Exodus 3:14 (KJV), Moses said to God, "Whom should I tell the people that sent me to set them free?"

God answered Moses, "I AM THAT I AM." The Lord explained, "Thou say unto the children of Israel I AM hath sent me unto you" (Exod. 3:14, AMP). "The Lord God of your fathers, the God of Abraham, of Isaac, and of Jacob, hath sent me unto you: This is my name forever, and this is my memorial unto all generations" (Exod. 3:15, KJV). *I am* being the same God who created the heaven and the earth out of nothing. Just by speaking, he created the earth we occupied and everything in it. Geneses 1:1–31 (AMP) shows the wonder and power of God. The great *I am* declares in Isaiah 45:18–23 (AMP), "For thus says the Lord, who created the heavens (He is the God who formed the earth and made it. He established it and did not create it a waste place but formed it to be inhabited). 'I am the Lord, and there is no one else. Declare and set forth your case; indeed, let them consult together, who has long since declared it? Is it not I, the Lord? And there is no other God beside Me, A righteous God and a Savior; there is none except Me. Turn to me and be saved, all the ends of the earth; for I am God, and there is no other, I have sworn by myself.'"

The same God takes the time to speak to Job during his trials and tribulations. Job is finally given his desire to have an audience with God. It is not what he expected. Speaking from a whirlwind, the Lord charges Job with darkening counsel by words without knowledge. A challenge is then made for Job to answer questions posed to him. A series of questions follows in rapid succession regarding the creation and nature that certainly contrast God's great power and wisdom with Job's limited ability and understanding (Job 38:1–46, AMP). Then the Lord answered Job out of the whirlwind and said,

"Where were you when I laid the foundation of the earth? Tell Me, if you have understanding, who set its measurement? Since you know. Or who stretched the line on it? On what were its bases sunk? Or who laid its cornerstone. Or who enclosed the sea with doors When, bursting forth, it went out from the womb; when I made a cloud its garment and thick darkness its swaddling band and I placed boundaries on it and set a bolt and doors. And I said, thus far you shall come, but no farther. And here shall your proud waves stop?"

God continued to question Job, "Have you ever in your life commanded the morning? And caused the dawn to know its place. That it might take hold of the ends of the earth, and the wicked be shaken out of it? Have you entered the springs of the sea or walked in the recesses of the deep? Has the gate of death been revealed to you? Or have you seen the gates of deep darkness? Have you understood the expanse of the earth? Tell Me if you know all this. Who has cleft a channel for the flood, or for a way for the thunderbolt to bring rain on a land without people, on a desert without a man in it, to satisfy the waist and desolate land and to make the seeds of grass to sprout? Has the rain a father? Or who has begotten the drop of dew? From whose womb has come the ice and the frost of heaven, who has given it birth? Water becomes hard like stone, and the surface of the deep is imprisoned. Can you lift up your voice to the cloud, so that an abundance of water will cover you? Can you send forth lightning that they may go and say to you, here we are? Who has put wisdom in the innermost being, or give understanding to the mind? Who can count the clouds by wisdom, or tip the water jars of the heavens, when the dust hardens into a mass and the clouds stick together?"

God ends his first discourse then with a repeated challenge for the one (i.e., Job) who contends with the Almighty and who rebukes God to answer these questions. Overwhelmed, Job admits his unworthiness and inability to answer. He admits he has spoken before but will do so no more (Job 38:1–40:5, AMP). Job's final response is to humbly acknowledge God's ability to do everything and that no purpose of his can be withheld from him. He also confesses that he has spoken of things he did not understand and beyond his ability to comprehend. Having now heard and seen God, Job abhors himself and repents (Job 42:1–6, AMP).

The transcendental aspect of God is greatly emphasized in the Old Testament. Moses warned people not to project an image of God or to personify him or draw a mental or physical image of him. It is considered a fatal mistake to create an image of God because it implies that man can put limits to what is limitless or measure what is eternal, absolute, and perfect with the yardstick of what is transient, relative, or imperfect. As such, he will lose his link to the divine.

Prayer to Know God

Heavenly Father, I come before you humbly, realizing I don't know much about you.

Lord, I desire to know you and to walk in the fullness of you.

Show me your ways, Lord; teach me your paths.

Guide me in your truth and teach me, for you are God my Savior,

and my hope is in you all day long.

Your word promises that to the one who knocks, the door will be opened.

I am knocking on your door, O Lord, ready to experience

the revelation of you.

Remember, O Lord, your compassion and unfailing love,

which you have shown from long ages past.

Do not remember the rebellious sins of my youth.

Open my eyes, my ears, and my heart to receive you as

you reveal yourself to me and not how I desire you to be.

Thank you, and I give you all praises, in Jesus's name,

Amen.

Endnotes

1   Michael Fackerell, "What Is Faith?" *Christian-Faith*, accessed February 1, 2014, https://www.christian-faith.com.

2   Fr. Edward Hopkins, LC, "Help My Unbelief!" *Catholic.net*, accessed February 1, 2014, http://catholic.net/op/articles/3770/cat/1185/help-my-un belief.html.

3   Ronald Youngblood, *Nelson's Illustrated Bible Dictionary*, "What Kind of God Is He?" (Nashville: Thomas Nelson, 1986).

4   Charles Hodge, *Systematic Theology*, 3 vols. (Reprint. London: James Clarke & Co. Ltd., 1960), 1:385.

5   Louis Berkhof, *Systematic Theology* (Louisville: GLH Publishing, 1932), 60.

6   Augustus Hopkins Strong, *Systematic Theology* (Toronto: University of Toronto Libraries, 1907), 279.

7   It is important to recognize that in speaking of God's knowledge, it does not imply a passive awareness of what will happen but a connection with his knowledge or foreknowledge that he has decreed all events. Compare William Greenough Thayer Shedd, *Dogmatic Theology* (Nashville: Thomas Nelson, 1888, Reprint. Phillipsburg: P & R Publishing, 2009), 1:353–58, 396–99.

8   Henry Clarence Thiessen, *Lectures in Systematic Theology* (Grand Rapids: Eerdmans, 1949), 82.

9   J. Oliver Buswell, *A Systematic Theology of the Christian Religion* (Grand Rapids: Zondervan, 1962), 72.

10 Charles Caldwell Ryrie, *The Grace of God* (Chicago: Moody Press, 1975), 9–26.

11 Shedd, *Dogmatic Theology*, 1:365–85.

CHAPTER THREE

GOD AS OUR FATHER

Before we can talk about faith in receiving what we pray for, I believe it is essential that we have a better understanding of why we should put our faith in God as our Father and what that means for us in fulfilling our lives' journey. Who you believe God to be will determine what you believe of yourself. There is the empowering verse that you can do all things through Christ who will give you strength. The mere idea that God listens to you or knows the number of the hairs on your head makes your value outstanding. If God values you, then of course it goes to follow that you should believe in that value. However, if you ask most people who they believe God to be, most will say, "He is the Father of Jesus Christ." But what can be added to this? It is my opinion that few in that group, including Christians, would be able to write even a half a page about the Father.

The greatest and most profound idea the human mind can ever conceivably entertain concerns the possibility of the existence of a personal God as Father. The sheer importance of man's response to this idea cannot be exaggerated, for it will not only govern our life down here, but it also determines our ultimate destiny. God as Father was mentioned by our Lord and Savior Jesus Christ well over two hundred times during his earthly ministry. Jesus spoke more about the Father than any other subject. Over the centuries, there have been many misconceptions about God and his true nature—legalistic religious leaders and angry earthly fathers who have by their lifestyles distorted God's true image and misrepresent him to us. As a result, we treat and trust God as we do our earthly father. Most of us see God as someone to go to for the things we need or someone to get us out of the troubles in which we find ourselves. But that is a limited view of what God as Father is to us.

It was God's original plan in the Garden of Eden that Adam and Eve would live all the days of their lives in the presence of a loving Father and would in turn reflect his love to their children. It was the Father's hope that each generation would grow up in the light of his love, never knowing a day of rejection or pain. However, love is not something that can be forced, so God gave Adam and Eve the privilege of free will. They had the freedom to trust God and stay in the garden or disobey him and leave.

In Genesis 3:23 (NKJV), we read that the latter happened, and because of their choice to become independent, they became separated from God. Because of Adam and Eve's actions, a new deadly disease called "sin" infected humanity. The world that God originally intended to be perfect and full of love was now wrought with pain and suffering because of the consequences of sin. Hurt people tend to hurt others, which is a legacy that has been passed on from generation to generation.

W. Graham Scroggie wrote that the outstanding truth that Christ taught about God is that he is Father. The term applied to him occurs 189 times in Matthew 44, Mark 4, Luke 17, and John 124 KJV.[1] According to Acts 17:24–25 (KJV), "He is the Father of all life. God that made the world and all things therein he giveth to all life, breath and all things." Psalm 19:1 (KJV) says, "The heaven declares the glory of God, and the firmament showed his handiwork." He tends and cares for vegetation. He causes the grass to grow for the cattle and herb for the service of man that he may bring forth food out of the earth. Matthew 6:28–30 (KJV) says, "If God so clothe the grass of the field, which today is and tomorrow is cast into the oven, shall he not much more clothe you?"

He tends and cares for nature; the high hills are a refuge for the wild goats and the rock for the conies. He makes darkness and its night, wherein all the beasts of the forest do creep forth. The young lions roar after their prey and seek their meat from God (Ps. 104:17–21, KJV). These wait all upon thee; that thou mayest give them their meat in due season (Ps. 104:27, KJV). He tends and cares for the weather, whatever the Lord pleased, that did he in heaven and in earth, in the seas, and all deep places. He causes the vapors to ascend from the ends of the earth; he makes lightning for the rain; he brings the wind out of his treasuries (Ps. 135:6–7, KJV).

Who covers the heaven with clouds, who prepares rain for the earth, who makes grass to grow upon the mountain? He gives snow like wool. He casts forth his ice like morsels. Who can stand before his cold? He sends out his word and melts them. He causes his wind to blow and the waters flow (Ps. 147:8, 16, 18, KJV). He tends and cares for the seasons. While the earth remains, seedtime and harvest, and cold and heat, and summer and winter, and day and night shall not cease (Gen. 8:22, KJV).

Nevertheless, he left not himself without witness, in that he did well, and gave us rain from heaven and fruitful seasons, filling our heart with food and gladness (Acts 14:17, AMP). Knowing God as our Father is a remarkable privilege; however, understanding the depth of our relationship with him is even better. Discover what it means to be a child of God, as author Kurt DeHaan helps us see the absolute perfection of our Heavenly Father. Find meaning, security, and perspective in every area of life when you put your trust in the one who is greater than life itself. He is the Father of all believers. While God is the creator of all men (Gen. 1:27; Eccles. 12:1; Acts 17:24–26, AMP), he is the Father only of believers.

What manner of love the Father hath bestowed upon us that we should be called the sons of God? (1 John 3:1, AMP) Abba is a word without an English synonym, at least not an exact one. Our best explanation is to say that it means *your very own father who loves you*. Everyone needs an *abba*-father, *don't you think?* God the Father was Abba to Jesus. He called the Father *Abba* when he was fearful the night before he was crucified. When you are in turmoil, God is there for you as *Abba*.

Since God created us for love, we are born with a great expectation to be loved and accepted. It is a scientific fact that babies who are not shown loving touch in the first few months of their lives can be physically and emotionally affected for the rest of their lives. Unfortunately, our parents could only express the love that they had first received from their parents. Thus, many of us have grown up with love deficits in our hearts. While we may know we are missing something, we may not be able to identify the emptiness that resides in the deepest part of our being. All we know is that we need to try and fill the emptiness somehow. Some try to fill this void in relationships, others in performance and success. Others seek to dull the emptiness with addictions. No matter what we do, if we do not encounter the real thing, we will always be left with a feeling of emptiness and unfulfillment.

There is only one place where we will find the true love and acceptance that we are looking for, and that is in a personal relationship with God. We were all born with a God-sized "hole in our soul" that can only be filled by God himself. Many of us have tried to fill this void with other things, but it just does not fit. The good news is that God wants to be in a relationship with us more than we want to be in one with him. The one who knows us before we were conceived (Jer. 1:4, AMP) and knits us together in our mother's womb (Ps. 139:13, AMP) wants to be our Father. While we are his offspring by creation, his desire is that we might become his children through redemption.

While we were still separated from him, the Father made a way for us to come home by sending his only son, Jesus Christ, to earth two thousand years ago to take care of the "sin" issue that had kept us separated. In obedience to his Father, Jesus bore upon himself the weight of our sin, nailing it to the cross so that we could be born into his wonderful family.

The last biblical story to consider is the Parable of the Prodigal Son. That son had a very loving father who forgave him for leaving home, leaving him, and making some immature and crazy choices. God the Father allows you to make choices that are sometimes immature and crazy as well. That is called free will. If you do not make the best choices, he does not cross you off his list but keeps his eyes open for your return.

Jesus is the way to the Father. His resurrection from the dead signaled the victory that would allow many sons and daughters to come into glory! In John 14:6 (AMP), Jesus says, "I am the way, the truth and the life, no man comes to the Father except through me." Our access to the Father is through Jesus alone. His sacrifice was the one and only price that could be paid for our redemption and restoration into the family of his wonderful Father. If we receive God's gift of his son, Jesus Christ, we receive the right to become children of God![2]

Three Things to Remember about God, Your Father

First, God the Father in the Old Testament is also the Abba of the New Testament. You may have heard that he is stern in the Old Testament and loving in the New, but that is just a rumor. Stern can be just another word for love sometimes.

Second, it is up to you to grow close. God the Father has never moved away. Any distance you experience is because you have backed away.

Third, you are on a journey. You will grow closer to God the Father. Begin today to keep that happy ending in mind. God the Father is with you on the journey, yet he is also the end of your journey—your destination.[3]

Would You like to Receive This Gift?

If you would like to accept this gift (eternal life in relationship with God), Jesus Christ has secured it for you. All you need to do is to tell God that you want to be saved. Believing saves you, and the words below might help you express your thoughts to God. It is not these exact words that will save you but the attitude of your heart toward God.[4]

Prayer to Accept or Reaffirm Your

Relationship with Jesus Christ

Father, I'm coming home. Please make me your child.

I turn from my sin.

I accept your forgiveness made possible through

Jesus Christ by his death and resurrection.

I place my faith and trust in Jesus alone.

I receive him as my Savior and Lord.

I want to follow and serve you.

Let today be the beginning of my new journey as your

child and a member of your family.

Thank you for making a way for me to come home.

In Jesus's name, I pray.

Amen.

Nothing will ever separate you from his love (Rom. 8:38, AMP). "For I am convinced that neither death nor life, neither angels nor demons, neither the present nor the future, nor any powers, neither height nor depth, nor anything in all creation, will be able to separate us from the love of God that is in Christ Jesus our Lord."

Steps to Help You in Your Walk with God

1. Get a Bible and read it each day.
2. Begin to cultivate "talking to God" in prayer each day.
3. Go to a church that believes and teaches the Bible.
4. Share your decision with a close friend.[5]

> *Let the whole earth sing to the Lord!*
> *Each day proclaim the good news that he saves.*
> *Publish his glorious deeds among the nations.*
> *Tell everyone about the amazing things he does.*
> *Great is the Lord! He is most worthy of praise!*
> *He is to be feared above all gods.*
> *The gods of other nations are mere idols,*
> *but the Lord made the heavens!*
> *Honor and majesty surround Him;*
> *strength and joy fill his dwelling.*
> *O nations of the world, recognize the Lord,*
> *recognize that the Lord is glorious and strong.*
> *Give to the Lord the glory he deserves!*
> *Bring your offering and come to worship him.*
> *Worship the Lord in all his holy splendor.*
>
> 1 Chronicles 16:23 29, NLT

Endnotes

1   W. Graham Scroggie, *A Guide to the Gospels: A Comprehensive Analysis of the Four Gospels* (Grand Rapids: Kregel Publications, 1948), 560.

2   Christopher M. Bellitto, PhD, "A Catholic Reads the Bible for the First Time," *Crux*, posted June 21, 2017, https://cruxnow.com/ commentary/2017/06/21/catholic-reads-bible-first time.

3   "Father's Love Letter." Father Heart Communications, 1999–2011, *FathersLoveLetter.com*.

4   Psalm 145:1. This psalm is an acrostic poem, the verses of which (including verse 13b) begin with the successive letters of the Hebrew alphabet.

5   Psalm 145:5. Dead Sea Scrolls and Syriac (see also Septuagint); Masoretic Text: On the glorious splendor of your majesty And on your wonderful works, I will meditate.

CHAPTER FOUR

WHAT IS FAITH?

W henever I would go through something unpleasant or difficult in my life, friends would say to me, "Keep the faith." I always thought they meant for me not to give up, so I did not. It gave me some sense of hope. As I got older and began to experience life in different dimensions and time, I realized faith is more than just not giving up. *So what is faith really?* As explained so beautifully by Pastor Bill Winston, founder and senior pastor of Living Word Christian Center, "Faith is the master key that will open every door. It will access every promise." Faith is what is needed to get you to the other side. Faith, in the simplest term, just believes God.

Do you see much faith in the world around you? Much of society today is secular-oriented and virtually devoid of faith. Since most people do not read the Bible, they do not know much about the true God. Many are not even sure there is a God. Others, although they believe in him, do not know what kind of God he is. This situation should not surprise us. After all, it is impossible for people to have living faith in a God they do not know or even know much about.

Faith is belief with strong conviction, firm belief in something for which there may be no tangible proof, complete trust, the opposite of doubt. Faith is being sure of what we hope for and certain of what we do not see; this is supernatural faith. Faith requires believing with your heart, not your head. From the inside, when you have faith, you have an anchor, direction, and purpose that other people, the ones who do not have faith, lack. *If you believe in nothing, you question everything, and where are you?* You are like a ship adrift without a destination. You have a crew but no captain, no pilot, no compass, and no charts. *You may end up in different waters from where you began, but to what purpose? What was the voyage for?*

The matter of faith changes all that. You know where you are going. If you die before you get there, at least you were going in the right direction, and your faith may give you the assurance that somehow the voyage isn't over; you'll continue in some other form. Faith lends meaning to an otherwise meaningless existence; it makes the whole matter of life worthwhile.

Faith is a seed of infinite potential. Faith holds all possibilities within it. Yet what does faith mean in our modern age of reason? Faith seems not quite natural to the modern mind. Mind is rational while faith is irrational. Mind is logical, faith illogical. Mind is doubtful while faith is doubt-free. In our modern culture, we have become more dedicated to doubt than to unbridled possibility. We are more committed to the calculations of the rational mind, than to the holistic wisdom of the spirit. Although the Christian faith is not based purely on evidence, it is supported by evidence.

Faith is not about turning off the brain and merely relying on the heart or squashing reason in favor of emotion. No, Christian faith is about seeking and knowing Jesus with all facets of the human character. It is not a "blind faith" as I once thought. It is a "calculated faith" based on a preponderance of the evidence. After spending numerous hours, days, and years reading and studying and after my personal encounter with the one called Jesus Christ, my personal conclusion of him is this: Jesus Christ is who he claims to be—the Son of God who came to this earth about two thousand years ago to offer true and lasting hope for mankind.

Have you ever considered *what faith is*? Or what process we go through to believe in something or someone? We need to understand the truth in our lives. Living by faith is not a minor thing; it is major. There is a difference in believing with our head and believing with our heart. Believing with our heart requires that we commit ourselves by taking action. Here is what faith is not: Faith is not religion. Many times, people say, "We have our faith." What they mean is this: "We have our religious ideas and doctrines, our traditions, our ways of doing things passed down through the generations. Don't you try to change them."

This is not the biblical idea of faith. Faith is not mental assent. It is not agreeing with your mind, "Yes, that is true." Many professing Christians believe mentally that the Bible is the Word of God, but this faith does not change the way they live. It is not a faith that can save (James 2:14, AMP). Even demons have that kind of faith. They know and believe that God exists (James 2:19, AMP) and tremble. They have no loving confidence in God.

Faith is not a way to manipulate God. It is not a power by which we make God do what we want when otherwise he would be unwilling to do that thing. It is not a kind of magic through which we make God into our servant! Faith is not hope or positive desire. Hope is good and relates to the future. Faith, however, takes the promise as done *now*. Many people have hope and are anxiously looking for results, but they lack the settled confidence and present assurance that faith has.

Are you aware of faith or belief in your everyday life? Think for a moment about the environment you live in. Are you sure the breath you take in will not damage your lungs and cause damage to your health? Yet you continue to take each breath and fill your lungs with air, which your body needs. Would you ever consider this to be "a leap of faith"? Of course you do. It's for this reason why you can sit on a chair without worrying if it will collapse under you, or if the bridge you ride over will hold the car, bus, or train you are in.

This type of faith is a natural one. You can see the object you are placing your faith in because you believe in the integrity and character of the engineers, contractors, and construction workers in doing the best job they can. Well, this is faith! You have faith in the characters and reputations of all the people involved in designing and constructing the bridge even though you have not met any of them.

In the general sense of the word, to have faith is to believe in something or someone, to fully trust, to be so confident that you base your actions on what you believe. To have faith is to be fully convinced of the truthfulness and reliability of that in which you believe. Faith in God then is having the kind of trust and confidence in God and in Christ that leads you to commit your whole soul to him as Savior (justifier, cleanser, healer, deliverer) and Lord (master, king).

The Bible says, "Now faith is the substance of things hoped for, the evidence of things not seen" (Heb. 11:1, NKJV). Faith is a spiritual substance. When you have this spiritual substance in you, it communicates to you a certain inner knowing that the thing you are hoping for is certainly established, even before you see any material evidence that it has happened. Faith is a spiritual force. Faith in God is a response to God's Word, which moves God to act.

Jesus says in Mark 11:23 (NKJV), "For assuredly I say to you, whoever SAYS to this mountain, 'Be removed and cast into the sea,' and does not doubt in his heart, but BELIEVES that those things he SAYS will be done, he will HAVE whatever he SAYS." Words mixed with the real, pure faith can and will move mountains or any other problem that we face. Hope is a condition for faith. Hope is "a positive unwavering expectation of good." Hope is for the mind (1 Thess. 5:8; Heb. 6:19), an anchor for the soul. It keeps us in the place where we can believe, but it is not in itself "faith." Yet without hope, there are no "things hoped for," and therefore there cannot be faith.

Through faith, we can know we have the answer to our prayer before we see anything change in the natural order (1 John 5:14–15, NKJV). Jesus said, "Therefore I say to you, whatever things you ask when you pray, believe that you receive them, and you will have them" (Mark 11:24, NKJV). God expects us, even commands us, to believe that God answers our petitions now the moment we ask him. We must believe that the response is immediately sent *when* we pray. Faith is like the confirmation slip in our hearts that the goods are on the way. We have that confirmation slip instantly from God. We sense it in our hearts the manifestation of those goods (the answer received) comes later if we are patient and do not throw away our confidence (Heb. 10:35–39; Heb. 6:12, NKJV).

Living in faith always has corresponding actions. We talk what we really believe, and we act according to what we really believe. The heroes of faith like Abraham were considered men of faith because they acted on what God showed them. They acted on their faith (Heb. 11:17–38; James 2:21–23, NKJV). To live in faith means to do and say what you believe is right, without doubting in your heart. Faith is a heart matter. Living a life of faith means never knowing where you are being led, but it does mean loving and knowing the one who is leading.

One of the biggest traps we fall into is the belief that if we have faith, God will surely lead us to success in the world. The final stage in the life of faith is the attainment of character, and we encounter many changes in the process. We feel the presence of God around us when we pray, yet we are only momentarily changed. We tend to keep going back to our everyday ways, and the glory vanishes.

A year or two into my relationship with Jesus, I had a vision, and in it the Spirit took me to the place where Jesus was nailed to the cross. He was alone; the other two men (the thieves) were not nailed next to him. I looked up at him, and when I noticed the hole in his side, I reached up with my four right fingers and placed them in his side. When I felt the wetness of his blood on my fingers, I woke up startled and said *these words*: "He really did die on the cross."

Why was I so surprised that Jesus really died on the cross? I heard it all my life, I had confessed it, and I was sure I believed that it did happen. *Did I believe it in my heart, or was it based on my intellect?* Is this the reason so many Christians are saved but have never been sanctified? Their lives have never been transformed. Jesus's death is nothing more than a religious exercise that makes us feel morally good.

Believing is not easy. It requires a constant recognition of our limitations, our inability to understand the "why" of so many occurrences and the "how" of so many challenges. This humble confession must come to rest always on the greatness of God's power and the comprehensiveness of his love. Jesus does not rebuke the struggle to believe but rather the lack of effort when we stop believing. The Father with one intense but short prayer did what the apostles failed to do: help my unbelief! *Do I believe that everything is possible if I only believe?*

The Way to Permanent Faith

According to Oswald Chambers, and I happened to believe it also, it is not that our faith is not real, but it is disordered and unfocused and not at work in the important realities of our lives. We are preparing for the trials and tribulations of life that are certainly not of our own choosing, but God engineers our circumstances to take us there. Until we have been through that experience, our faith is sustained only by feelings and by blessings. Dark times are allowed and come to us through the sovereignty of God. Are we prepared to be separated from the outward evident blessings of God? Until Jesus is truly our Lord, we each have goals of our own that we serve. Our faith is real, but it is not yet permanent, and God is in no hurry. If we are willing to wait, we will see God pointing out that we have been interested only in his blessings instead of in God himself.

A year ago, the reality of my faith was tested in ways I never could have anticipated. What I found out through this very painful process is that my faith was based on my experiences and not on God's revelation of truth. God allowed this very dark period in my journey to show me that faith based on experience is not faith, but faith based on God's revelation of truth is the only faith there is. I had so many amazing experiences with God that I would have never thought

I would question my faith or my trust in him, and that is exactly what happened. Lost in my troubles and determined to fix them myself, I went further into the abyss. The deeper I went, the less I could hear from God. I lost my first love; I could not find him. Everything I did and every choice I made took me further away from him.

How could this be happening to me? I am the girl who had that third heaven experience, not once but twice. God took me in the Spirit and showed me amazing things, yet I found out that I did not trust God in all the areas of my life. For healing, absolutely. I have no doubt about the power of God to heal me. On two separate occasions, I was told I had a major physical problem. I would put my hands on the particular area and repeat Isaiah 53:4–6 (NKJV): "Surely our griefs He Himself bore and our sorrows He Carried; Yet we ourselves esteemed Him stricken. Smitten of God, and afflicted, But He was pierced through for our transgressions, He was crushed for our iniquities; The chastening for our well-being fell upon Him. And by His scourging we are healed." Each time I returned to the doctor; the problem was no longer there. God healed me because I believed.

My faith in God's healing power is unwavering, thus healing would manifest in my body or for anyone I prayed for. I have even witnessed someone rise from the dead. God has shown me his awesome powers, yet when it came to my finances, I could not let it go totally to God. The more I depended on my own abilities and knowledge, the worst my financial situation would get. I blamed God for every bad decision I made, and when I was disappointed in myself, I transferred it to him. It got so bad that I accused God of not being real. "I was deceived," I said, "to believe you, God, were real." When I tried to pray, I could not. I was so twisted my prayer partners would pray for me and encourage me, but it was not working for me anymore.

Finally, when I thought I could not take it anymore, he came and pulled me out of my depressive state by showing me once again who he is and that he will always be for me, the Father who loves me and wants the best for me always. God did not fix my financial problems immediately. He took me back to the scriptures in the Bible that tell of God's character and his attributes to remind me of what I already knew but somehow had forgotten.

It is amazing how we tend to respond to crises in our lives when we do not get the answers we seek right away. *Can God's love continue to hold fast, even when everyone and everything around us seems to be saying that his love is a lie, and there is no such thing as justice? Can we believe in the love of God but also be more than conquerors, even while we are being starved?* Either God is a deceiver, or some extraordinary thing happened to someone who holds on to the love of God when the odds are totally against them. Logic is silent in the face of each of these things, which comes against us. Only one thing can account for it, faith, and the love of God in Christ Jesus.

There is only one way to develop and grow spiritually in our faith, and that is through focusing and concentrating on God. In essence, Jesus was saying, "Do not worry about being of use to others, simply believe in Me." In other words, pay attention to the source, and out of you "will flow rivers of living waters" (John 7:38, NKJV). We cannot discover the source of our natural life through common sense and reasoning, and Jesus is teaching here that growth in our spiritual life comes not from focusing directly on it but from concentrating on our Father in heaven.

Our Heavenly Father knows our circumstances, and we will grow spiritually, just as "the lilies of the field." If we are living a life of faith, we will exercise our right to waive our rights and let God make our choice for us. God sometimes allows us to get into a place of testing, where our own welfare would be the appropriate thing to consider if we were not living the life of faith. But if we are, we will joyfully waive our right and allow God to make our choice for us. Whenever our rights become the guiding factor of our lives, it dulls our spiritual insight.

The greatest enemy of the life of faith in God is not sin, said Oswald Chambers, but good choices, which are not quite good enough. The good is always the enemy of the best. It is not only wrong to worry but also unbelief. Worrying means we do not believe that God can look after the practical details of our lives, that we can do a better job than him.

What did Jesus say would choke the Word he put in us? Is it the devil? No, "the cares of the world" (Matt. 13:22, NKJV). "I will not trust what I cannot see," and that is where unbelief begins. *The only cure for unbelief is obedience to the Spirit. Getting to faith is easy; staying there is where the challenge comes, it can be done.* You will need to know about the one you are placing your faith in—his attributes, his character, and what he says about you.

Go back and read chapters two and three. Like any relationship, you must spend time with God to get to know him. You can do this through prayer and reading his word, committing your life to him, and walking in obedience. Many of us do not continue to grow spiritually because we prefer to choose based on our rights instead of relying on God to make the choice for us. I know it is difficult, but we must learn to walk according to the standard that has its eyes focused on God. And God says to us, as he did to Abram, "Walk before Me…" (Gen. 17:11, NKJV).

Why Must We Believe God?

Why must we believe God? Hebrews 11:6 says, "But without faith it is impossible to please God, for he who comes to God must believe that He is, and that He is a rewarder of those who diligently seek Him." Romans 14:23 (NKJV) says, "Whatever is not of faith is sin," and God hates sin. When we do not believe God, we treat him like he is a liar. Remember that he is everywhere and sees all things. He is hurt when we act like he does not exist or that he will not do what he promised to do. Only when we have confidence in God and his word can we please him.

Michael Fackerell of Christian-Faith says, "Lack of faith leads to lack of obedience." God's commands can only really be fulfilled through faith. Without confidence in God's promises, a man will never really do what God says. Lack of obedience in God's eyes is rebellion. Such lack of obedience dishonors God and surely deserves to be punished. "The just shall live by faith" (Rom. 1:17, NKJV). We must live by faith to be considered by God "right" and "correct." Otherwise, we stand condemned.

Those who do not believe in God inevitably believe in something else—either religious tradition; their understanding of science; what the latest magazine says; what their next-door neighbor, the education system, or the mass media tells them; or a combination of all these things. God is not impressed. "Professing to be wise, they became fools" (Rom. 1:22, NKJV). In fact, those who do not fully believe in God end up believing the devil somewhere along the line. It is very possible to believe what the devil says without even believing that he exists! Satan is speaking through so many philosophies and religions without openly declaring himself. Not too many know they are trusting the words of Satan and his demons. God is therefore righteous in expecting us to believe in him and what he says. Who is better qualified to tell us the truth and help us find answers?

OK, now what? I intellectually believe, by a preponderance of the evidence, that God exists, that the Bible is true, and that Jesus is his Son. *How does this affect me? What is faith, as far as it concerns me? Is he reliable for me today? Can I really put my twenty-first-century faith in him?* Well, I think even more so as our world is changing so very rapidly, for better or for worse. As technology keeps changing and improving our quality of life, this allows us to have more time to ponder our world around us. *Let us ask ourselves honestly, what do we believe in, and why do we believe it?* Are we basing our faith on an institution or on the character of someone? We have seen over the years many institutions and religions come, change, and go. But the character of our Heavenly Father does not change. He is our eternal Father, and as the men and women of the Old and New Testaments had put their trust in him back then, so can we now in the twenty-first century.

MAURINE MCFARLANE

Prayer of Faith

Heavenly Father, I come before you in the name of Jesus Christ.

I do believe. Help me overcome my unbelief!

O my God, I trust in thee; let me not be ashamed,

let not my enemies triumph over me.

Lord, grant me an increase of faith!

Help me to see you present and active in my everyday life.

Lord, I do believe. Help me overcome my unbelief!

Jesus, in your love for me you know my every need

even before I am aware of it. I believe in your ability to provide

for my daily need even when I am fearful that you can't or won't.

I do believe, Lord. Help me overcome my unbelief!

I believe that you can do all things in me, according to your own will.

I believe your will is committed to what is best for me.

Teach me to pray and work with great faith and trust in you.

Lord, I do believe. Help me overcome my unbelief!

In Jesus's name,

Amen.

CHAPTER FIVE

"SIN"—OUR NATURAL NATURE

I did not write this chapter on sin so you or I could feel bad about ourselves, but so we can have a greater understanding of the depth of God's love for us, the importance of the sacrificed and why it was necessary for him to send his only begotten Son to the cross in exchange for us. The more we know, the more aware we will be, and the more aware we are of our habits that can destroy us, the less likely we will repeat them.

Many who refuse to admit the existence of sin are stubbornly adamant in their position. They think their opposition to the presence of sin can neither be controverted nor challenged. The Bible, however, declares sin's existence, and the human heart displays it. Sin is not a myth; it is not a figment of the mind; sin is a fact. Not being reconciled to the fact of sin, not recognizing it and refusing to deal with it produces all the disasters in life. If you refuse to agree with the fact that there is wickedness and selfishness, something downright hateful and wrong in human beings, then when it attacks your life, instead of reconciling yourself to it, you will compromise with it and say that it is of no use to battle against it.

For my own enlightenment, I had to spend some time studying this topic. I needed to understand my own behavior, why I did what I did and sometimes continues to do. Through the work and teaching of Dr. Arnold G. Fruchtenbaum from Ariel Ministries, I would get the answers I seek. I am sharing with you what I have learned in the hope that you too will find the answers you seek.

The first thing to understand is this: sin is a fundamental relationship; it is not wrongdoing but wrong being. It is a deliberate and determined independence from God. We must recognize that sin is a fact of life, not just a shortcoming. Sin is a blatant mutiny against God, and either sin or God must die in our lives. The first thing Jesus Christ confronted in people was the heredity of sin, and it is because we have ignored this in our presentation of the gospel that the message of the gospel has lost its sting and its explosive power. The revealed truth of the Bible is not that Jesus Christ took on himself our fleshly sins but that he took on himself the heredity of sin that no man can even touch.

The Explanation of Sin

What is sin? When one seeks the answer to this question in the many and varied definitions of men, we are left somewhat confused. There is a difference between the way God describes and explain sin and the way that men describe and explain sin.

The word "sin" is found hundreds of times in the Bible in both Old and New Testaments. Its first mention is in Genesis 4:7 (NKJV), where it is said to have been lurking at the door of the world's first murderer, Cain. The second reference is found in Genesis 18:20 (NKJV), where it causes the fiery and fearsome destruction of Sodom. The final mention is in Revelation 18:5 (NKJV), where it brings down the full wrath of an angry God upon the political and economic systems of this entire world.[1]

According to Dr. Arnold G. Fruchtenbaum, sin, on some occasions, is to be distinguished from evil. For example, sin is not always the exact same thing as evil. We often refer to cyclones, floods, fires, earthquakes, and such as evil, and well, they may be. But these cannot be called sin. This fact should be understood as many Christians have been troubled and confused over the words of God in Isaiah 45:7 (NKJV), where we read, "I form the light, and create darkness: I make peace, and create evil: I the Lord do all these things."

Here the Hebrew word *ra* is used, which can also be translated to "calamity." Thus, while we read of God creating evil, the scriptures assure us he does not create sin. "For He hath made Him to be sin for us, who knew no sin; that we might be made the righteousness of God in Him" (2 Cor. 5:21, NKJV). "In hope of eternal life, which God, that cannot lie, promised before the world began" (Titus 1:2, NKJV). "For we have not a High Priest which cannot be touched with the feeling of our infirmities; but was in all points tempted like as we are, yet without sin" (Heb. 4:15, NKJV). "Who did not sin, neither was guile found in his mouth" (1 Pet. 2:22, NKJV). "And ye know that He was manifested to take away our sins; and in Him is no sin" (1 John 3:5, NKJV).[1]

No man should ever think that he comes anywhere near the standard set by God. God has demanded absolute perfection, and no matter how one measures himself, he falls far short. Some men measure themselves based on human intelligence, some by educational attainment, some by financial success, some by cultural environment, and others by religious performance. But God refuses to accept man on any of these grounds. He has established his perfect standard, and by that standard, he measures every man.

The divine verdict in every instance has been the same— "You have come short, and you have missed the mark." And when the best of men have done their best, our Lord would challenge each with the words "Which of you by taking thought can add one cubit unto his stature?" (Matt. 6:27, NKJV). However much the difference that is lacking, no man can by himself raise himself to meet God's moral standard. "For all have sinned, and come short of the glory of God" (Rom. 3:23, NKJV). Yes, all without exception. "We have before proved both Jews and Gentiles, that they are all under sin" (Rom. 3:9, NKJV); that is, both Jew and Gentile have missed the mark. From these verses, we are told that the basic reason for the incarnation of God's Son was to deal with this terrible thing called sin.[1]

The Definition and Meaning of Sin

There are two words in the Greek New Testament that most closely define sin. *Hamartema* means to *miss the mark*. Missing the mark implies hitting the wrong mark. It means to come short of the glory that God intended for man to reach. Every man has failed to do what he ought; therefore, the term is fittingly applied to sins of omission. Every man can be charged with the sin of the Pharisees whom our Lord charged with leaving undone the things they ought to have done (Matt. 23:23; Luke 11:42, NKJV).

The Bible says, "Therefore to him that knows to do good, and doeth it not, to him it is sin" (James 4:17, KJV). You see, sinning is not limited to the doing and saying things that are wrong, but it extends to our failure to do what in God's standard is perfectly right, missing that mark, falling short of the honor and worth of Almighty God (Rom. 3:23, NKJV). It is the only explanation why Jesus Christ came to earth, and it is the explanation of the grief and sorrow of life. Always beware of any assessment of life, which does not recognize the fact that there is sin.[2]

Parabasis: "To overstep a forbidden line"

According to this definition, sin occurs when man deliberately (or accidentally) steps over the line of the law of God. The basic meaning is "to revolt" or "to refuse subjection to rightful authority." The law has a relationship to sin; it gives the standard to show what sin is. Romans 4:15 says, "Because the law brings about wrath; for where there is no law there is no transgression." However, the word "law" does not always refer only to the Ten Commandments. Sin is called transgression of the law, but not all sin is transgression of the Ten Commandments. The law keeps one in check; it is a boundary line. Romans 5:13 (NKJV) states, "For until the law sin was in the world, but sin is not imputed when there is no law." This shows there was sin previously without the Ten Commandments, which means that God gave numerous commands before; these are spoken laws to those he instructed.[2]

History shows this to be true; for example, the angels sinned (2 Pet. 2:4, NKJV), which means, as it states, they left their assigned place that God gave. Adam sinned not by breaking the Ten Commandments (Rom. 5:12). The only commandments God gave Adam were to keep the garden, be fruitful, and not eat from the tree of knowledge of good and evil. These texts have no reference to the Ten Commandments. The Sodomites sinned (Gen. 13:13, NKJV) and "the Gentiles which have not the law" sinned (Rom. 2:12–14, NKJV). We can see that sin is something more than a violation of the Decalogue.

In the New Testament, John says, "All unrighteousness is sin" (1 John 5:17, NKJV). A neglect to do good is sin (James 4:17, NKJV). Unbelief is sin (Rom. 14:23, NKJV), but none of these are a transgression of the Decalogue. There are numerous wrongs that the Decalogue does not address. God writes to us that the law came so we may know how to measure sin specifically.[2]

Through time God continued to give commands. "Moreover the law entered that the offense might abound, but where sin abounded, grace abounded much more" (Rom. 5:20, NKJV). The law's intent was to increase one's ability to sin, to exaggerate its practice so it would be evident. According to Romans 3:20 (NKJV), "For through the Law {comes} the knowledge of sin." This is the same law Paul speaks about that condemns and makes one guilty. It includes the Ten Commandments and anything else contrary to God. The law was given to show man could not meet the requirements of God. If you put yourself under the law you will sin, it has no power. It is for those who operate in the flesh to know they fall short of his standard.[2]

Simple Definition of Sin

The simple definition that includes all the above elements is "sin is anything contrary to the character of God." That simple definition covers all the various elements: selfishness is contrary to the character of God, transgression of known law is contrary to the character of God, a wrong attitude and desire of self are contrary to God's character, unbelief is contrary to God's character, and voluntary disobedience of an explicit command of God is contrary to God's character. A slightly more detailed definition would be "sin is any lack or want of conformity to the character of God, whether it is an act, a disposition, or a state."[3]

The Essential Nature of Sin

There are ten things that should be noted about "The Essential Nature of Sin":

First Essential Nature of Sin: Sin is a specific type of evil.

Second Essential Nature of Sin: Sin is a lack of conformity to or a transgression of the law of God. It is a failure to do what the law demands (James 4:17, NKJV). To fail in one point of the law is to be guilty of breaking the whole law (Gal. 3:10; James 2:10, NKJV). The lack of ability to obey is not the measure of obligation or test of what sin is. Sin is there whether one feels he is able to keep the law.

Third Essential Nature of Sin: Sin a principle or a nature as well as an act (Matt. 15:19, NKJV). As an act, sin produces guilt; as a principle, sin produces pollution (Jer. 17:9; Luke 6:45, NKJV). Because sin is both a nature and a principle as well as an act, it produces a sixfold result.

Sixfold Result of Sin

1. The understanding of man is darkened (Rom. 1:31; 1 Cor. 22:14; Eph. 4:18, NKJV).
2. It produces an evil and vain imagination (Gen. 6:5, 12; Rom. 1:21, NKJV).
3. It produces vile affections or passion (Rom. 1:26–27, NKJV).
4. It produces corrupt speech (Eph. 4:29, NKJV).
5. It produces a defiled mind and conscience (Titus 1:15, NKJV).
6. It produces an enslave and depraved will (Rom. 7:18–19, NKJV).

Fourth Essential Nature of Sin: It is selfishness because ultimately sin emphasizes oneself as being primary over and against the primacy of God.

Fifth Essential Nature of Sin: The thing about the essential nature of sin is that sin is also lawlessness (1 John 3:4, NKJV). It is lawlessness in that sin contains the aspect of a failure to live in accordance with the law and commandments of God.

Sixth Essential Nature of Sin: Sin has an absolute character; it is not some vague influence (Matt. 10:32–33, 12:30; Luke 11:13; James 2:10, NKJV).

Seventh Essential Nature of Sin: Sin always has a relationship to God and his will (Rom. 1:32, 2:12–14, 4:15, 5:13; James 2:9–10, NKJV).

Eighth Essential Nature of Sin: Sin includes both guilt and pollution. Concerning guilt, it makes man liable for punishment (Rom. 3:19, 5:18; Eph. 2:3, NKJV). Concerning pollution, all man is guilty of moral pollution in Adam because they are born of a corrupt nature. Moral pollution means that there is a disposition toward evil (Job 14:4; Isa. 6:5; Jer. 17:9; Rom. 8:5–8; Eph. 4:17–19, NKJV).

Ninth Essential Nature of Sin: Sin has its roots in the heart. Sin influences the intellect, the emotion, and the will, and it finds expression through the body (Prov. 4.23, Jer. 17.9, Matt. 15:19–20; Luke 6:45; Heb. 3:12, NKJV).

Tenth Essential Nature of Sin: Sin does not consist of an outward act only. There is a three-stage progression to a sinful act:[3]

1. Sin consists of a sinful state (Matt. 5:22, 28, NKJV).
2. The sinful state becomes the basis for sinful habits (Rom. 7:7, NKJV).
3. These sinful habits result in sinful deeds (Rom. 7:17, 24, NKJV). (3)

The sin nature or the original sin refers to the first sin committed by human beings as is emphasized in Romans 5:19 (NKJV). Adam's sin brought original guilt and original pollution. This original pollution caused total depravity and inability so that even man's best works are still radically defective. The term "original sin" can refer to Adam's sin. Because it originated with Adam and flows from the first parents, Adam and Eve, everyone inherits this sin nature.

It is also called sin nature because it is the original of all sins; therefore, all people commit the acts of sin because of their sin nature. Every person enters the human race as a sinner and commits the acts of sin because they are sinners. Adam and Eve are the only two people who ever became sinners by sinning. All their descendants (us) sin because we are sinners. Only Adam and Eve died spiritually by sinning; we, their descendants, are born spiritually dead. Because we are born with a sin nature, we commit the act of sin.[3]

Furthermore, the sin nature is a corruption of the very essence of the soul. The sin nature is not an essential element of the immaterial part of man. Adam and Eve live for a period without a sin nature. Jesus existed all his life without a sin nature. The sin nature is a capacity to do all these things, both good and bad, which in no way commends a person to God.[3]

The concept of the sin nature is taught heavily throughout both the Old and New Testaments. In the Old Testament, the sin nature is spoken of in Genesis 6:5, 8:21; Job 15:14, 16; Psalm 58:1–3, 94:11, 130:3, 143:2; Isaiah 64:6; and Jeremiah 13:23, 16:12, 17:19. In the New Testament, the sin nature is spoken of in Matthew 7:11, 12:34, 15:19; Romans 16:6:20; 1 Corinthians 2:14; Ephesians 4:18; Colossians 2:13; and 1 Peter 4:2 (NKJV). From these many examples in both the New and Old Testaments, it is clear that the Bible does indeed teach the concept of the sin nature and original sin.[3]

The Transmission of the Sin Nature

The sin nature is transmitted by what is called "mediate transmission." This means that it comes from Adam to all his descendants through the parents. It does not come directly from Adam to everyone. Rather, it comes from Adam, through all his descendants, through our parents, to us. Conversely children inherit their sin nature from their parents, and parents from their parents, all the way back to Adam (Ps. 51:5; Eph. 2:3, NKJV).[4]

The Penalty for the Sin Nature

The penalty for the sin nature and original sin involves two things.

The first penalty is total depravity. This does not mean that every man is as bad as he can be. Rather, total depravity means "the unmeritorious state of man before God." None of man's works carries any merit before God.

The second penalty for the sin nature is spiritual death. Because man inherits the sin nature upon conception, he is born spiritually dead (Gen. 2:17; 1 Cor. 2:14; Eph. 2:1, 5, NKJV). The sin nature is not dead, but the believer is dead to it in that he is no longer obligated to obey its demands as he was before he was saved.

The penalties for the sin nature carry with them four specific results.

The first result is that there is a corruption of the very nature of the soul, in that the soul is rendered spiritually dead.

The second result is that there is the loss of original righteousness. When Adam and Eve were created, they had original righteousness, but they lost it when they sinned. Now the inclination of man is toward evil.

The third result is that it is the nature of sin to include guilt and corruption. Guilt refers to the outward aspect of sin; corruption refers to the inward aspect of sin.

The fourth result is that the sin nature retains its character even in the believers; that is the reason believers still sin.[5]

Personal Sin

So what is personal sin? And how is it different from our sin nature? The key verse that deals with the concept of personal sin is Romans 3:23 (NKJV): "for all have sinned and fall short of the glory of God." Personal sin means the acts of sin committed by individuals before they believe on (Yeshua) Jesus as their Savior or Messiah. While the sin nature is inward, personal sin is outward; it is the act of sin. These acts of sin are committed because man is by nature a sinner, because he inherited the sin nature. Therefore, personal sins are the act of sin committed by individuals before they accept Jesus as their messiah. These may be willful acts, or they may be acts committed out of ignorance, but they are still act of sin. Personal sin includes everything in daily life that is against or fails to conform to the character of God.[6]

The Transmission of Personal Sin

Again, personal sin originates from the sin nature; it is because he has a sin nature that man commits the acts of sin. The sin nature is transmitted from Adam through the parents. The sin nature is inherited from parents upon conception, and then the acts of sin are committed because of that sin nature. The consequences of personal sin may affect one's descendants for four generation because, according to Exodus 34:6–7 (NKJV), the justice of God sometimes requires that the sin of the fathers be visited upon the children, and upon the children's children, upon the third and fourth generations.[6]

The Meaning of Imputed Sin

"Impute" means "to reckon to one's account." It means to attribute or to reckon something to someone. The Bible speaks of three great imputations. The first imputation is the imputation of Adam's sin to humans. The second imputation is the imputation of man, the sin of man to the Messiah; this occurred on the cross. The third imputation is the imputation of the righteousness of the Messiah to the believer; this happens when one believes. We will focus on the first big imputation, which is the foundation of the other two.

The first great imputation is when Adam's sin was imputed to humans. All mankind is viewed as having participated in Adam's disobedience, and therefore, all mankind carries the same guilt. Man is not only guilty of his own personal sins because he has the sin nature, but man is also guilty because he is viewed as having participated in Adam's sin. From the biblical perspective, in Romans 5:12–21 (NKJV), God sees all humanity as being "in Adam." Thus, all men are reckoned as being guilty, not only of our own sin but also of Adam's sin. The key verse in this passage is verse 12: "Therefore, as through one-man sin entered the world, and death through sin; and so, death passed unto all men, for that all sinned."[6]

Transmission of Imputed Sin

Imputed sin is transmitted by the theological term "natural headship." Natural headship means that imputed sin is transmitted immediately from Adam to us individually. While the sin nature was transmitted by mediate transmission in that it went from Adam through our parents to us individually, imputed sin, however, is by means of immediate transmission in that it goes from Adam directly to each of us. In scripture, this concept is known as "seminal relationship." One example of seminal relationship is found in Hebrews 7:9–10 (NKJV): "And, so to say, through Abraham even Levi, who received tithes, has paid tithes; for he was yet in the loins of his father, when Melchizedek met him."

The background to the passage is Genesis 14, where Abraham paid tithes to Melchizedek. The author of the book of Hebrews points out that when Abraham paid tithes, Levi, who was a descendant of Abraham, was also viewed as having paid tithes to Melchizedek by means of imputation through seminal relationship. Levi was not even born when that event occurred.

Nevertheless, because he was in the lions of his father, Abraham, Levi was viewed as having paid tithes to Melchizedek.

The entire human race was "in the lions of Adam" because of that seminal relationship. When Adam sinned, all humanity is viewed as having participated in the sin. Adam's sin is imputed to all mankind because it is also reckoned as being ours (Rom. 5:12, NKJV). It means that death passed upon all men because all sinned "in Adam," who was the natural head of the human race by virtue of seminal relationship.[7]

The Penalty for Imputed Sin

According to Romans 5:12, the penalty for imputed sin is physical death. This was already taught in the Old Testament in Genesis 3:19. This is also taught in the New Testament in Romans 5:14 and 1 Corinthians 15:20–23 (NKJV), specifically the phrase in verse 22: "For as in Adam all die."[7]

The Remedy for Imputed Sin

The remedy for imputed sin is that third great imputation mention earlier, the imputation righteousness of the Messiah. This is taught in the same context as imputed sin. In the context of Romans 5:12–21 (NKJV), verse 21 states, "That, as sin reigned in death, even so might grace reigned through righteousness unto eternal life through Jesus Christ our Lord," which can be found in 2 Corinthians 5:21 (NKJV). The verse begins with the words "Him who knew no sin, he made to be sin on our behalf." This is dealing with the second great imputation of the sin of man upon the Messiah. The verse then states that we might become the righteousness of God in him. This truth is also taught in 1 Corinthians 15:20–26, 54–56 (NKJV). Verse 22 states, "For as in Adam all die, so also in the Messiah shall all be made alive."[7]

The Law

I have been "born again" going on over twenty years. When it comes to the laws of the Bible, Old Testament versus New Testament, understanding which laws we are no longer under versus the ones we should recognize for our time always leave me confused. Before I go any further, let me explain what being "born again" means. Jesus called being born again a new birth. He also called it being saved. The phrase "born again" literally means "born from above."

Nicodemus had a real need; he needed a change of his heart, a spiritual transformation. New birth, being born again, is an act of God whereby eternal life is imparted to the person who believes (2 Cor. 5:17; Titus 3:5; 1 Pet. 1:3; 1 John 2:29, 3:9, 4:7, 5:1–4, 18; John 1:12–13, NKJV), indicating that being "born again" also carries the idea of "becoming children of God" through trust in the name of Jesus Christ.[8]

The question logically comes, "Why does a person need to be born again?" The apostle Paul in Ephesians 2:1 (NKJV) says, "And you He made alive, who were dead in trespasses and sins." To the Romans, he wrote, "For all have sinned and fall short of the glory of God" (Rom. 3:23, NKJV). Sinners are spiritually "dead"; when they receive spiritual life through faith in Christ, the Bible likens it to a rebirth. Only those who are born again have their sins forgiven and have a relationship with God.

Unbelievable as it may seem, many good churchgoing people have never had that experience. They have a mental understanding of the scriptures. They even know that Jesus is the Son of God. Yet their nature has never been changed. They have not been born again because they have not received Jesus in a personal way as their very own Savior and as the Lord of their lives. How can a subject matter such as the law that is so fundamental to how we function and behavior as believers not taught with more clarity?

I must pause and give thanks to the Lord. In writing this book, he is taking me through each step to have a greater understanding of who he is, what is important to him, and why. Understanding the different laws that God laid out for humanity will give us a closer connection to him, which also helps our faith to become more permanent. Dr. Arnold G. Fruchtenbaum's teaching on the law has given me a greater understanding, and I pray it does the same for you.[8]

The Nature of the Law

Dr. Arnold G. Fruchtenbaum focuses on five areas of the law, which he calls the Usages of the Word. **First**, he explained what the word "law" is sometimes used to refer to the Mosaic law. Most of the times the Bible uses the term, it is a reference to the Law of Moses (6:14–15; Gal. 4:4, NKJV). **Second** usage is the term "elemental law" or "moral law." This is not a specific commandment of Moses as such but merely the moral law, basic law, of element law found in our society (Rom. 4:15, 5:13, NKJV). **Third** usage is the term "civil law" found in Daniel 6:8, 12 (NKJV). **Fourth** usage of the word "law" is the revealed will of God, such as in Psalm 119:18 (NKJV). **Fifth** usage of the word "law" in scripture is a principle of operation; this is found in Romans 7:21, 8:2 (NKJV). **Sixth** usage of the word "law" is the law of the Messiah, Jesus Christ.[8]

Like the Law of Moses, the law of the Messiah contains a body of specific commandments such as in 1 Corinthians 9:21 and Galatians 6:2 (NKJV). In the New Testament alone, the word "law" is found a total of 209 times; most of these are found in two books, Romans and Galatians. In the book of Romans, the word is used 27 times; in the book of Galatians, it is used 30 times. Throughout the rest of the New Testament, it is used another 102 times.

Just focusing on the New Testament alone, the word "law" is used in thirteen different ways: the law of works (Rom. 3:27, NKJV), the law of faith (Rom. 3:27, NKJV), the law of God (Rom. 7:22, 25, 8:7, NKJV), the law of the mind (Rom. 7:23, NKJV), the law of sin (Rom. 7:23, 25, 8:2 (NKJV), the law of the Spirit of life in Christ Jesus (Rom. 8:2, NKJV), the law of death (Rom. 8:2, NKJV), the law of righteousness (9:31, NKJV), the law of Christ (Gal. 6:2, NKJV), the law of the Jews (Acts 25:8, NKJV), the law of liberty (James 1:25, 2:12, NKJV), the law of the Lord (Luke 2:23–24, 39, NKJV), and the law of Moses (Luke 2:22, 24:44; John 7:23; Acts 13:39, 15:5, 28:23; 1 Corinthians 9:9, NKJV).[8]

It is important that we understand that although there is a wide variety of the usage of the word "law" throughout the Old and the New Testaments, the primary usage in both testaments is for the Law of Moses. Violation of any law that is applied by God to man results in sin, whether it is the moral law, the Law of Moses, or the law of the Messiah.

The simple meaning of law according to Dr. Arnold G. Fruchtenbaum carries four implications. The first implication is there is a lawgiver. That lawgiver is God. The second implication is that there is a subject who receives the law and must obey it. Man is the subject, and he must obey any law given by the lawgiver as applicable to him. The third implication is that this law is an expression of the divine will. Because the lawgiver is God himself, what he hands down as law is the expression of his divine will. The fourth implication is that he can enforce his will; he has the power to enforce his will and may use his power whenever he deems necessary.[8]

The Extreme Concerning Law

There are two extremes concerning the law and implications. One extreme is called antinomianism, which teaches that believers are not subject to any law at all. Most antinomians use verses that teach that the believers are no longer subject to the Law of Moses, which is true. However, believers are still subject to a law, and that is the law of the Messiah. The apostle Paul dealt with the issue of antinomianism in Romans 6:1–2 (NKJV): "What shall we say, then? Shall we go on sinning so that grace may increase? By no means! We died to sin; how can we live in it any longer?"

The most frequent attack on the doctrine of salvation by grace alone is that it encourages sin. People may wonder, "If I am saved by grace and all my sins are forgiven, why not sin all I want?" That thinking is not the result of true conversion because true conversion yields a greater desire to obey, not a lesser one. God's desire and our desire when we are regenerated by his Spirit is that we strive not to sin. Out of gratitude for his grace and forgiveness, we want to please him. God has given us his infinitely gracious gift in salvation through Jesus (John 3:16; Rom. 5:8, NKJV). Our response is to consecrate our lives to him out of love, worship, and gratitude for what he has done for us (Rom. 12:1–2, NKJV). Antinomianism is unbiblical in that it misapplies the meaning of God's gracious favor.

The second extreme is legalism. Legalism is adding man-made laws to the laws that God has given and making these man-made laws mandatory as well. Both antinomianism and legalism are wrong. The balance is that the believer must obey the rules of God that are applicable to him in this age.[8]

Types of Law

There are two major types of categories of law.

1. Elemental Law

Elemental law means a law that is wrought into the elements, substances, and forces of rational and irrational creatures. These elemental laws become physical or natural laws, such as the law of gravity, the three laws of thermodynamics, and others. The elemental law that is wrought into the constitution of rational and free beings becomes moral law. All humanity has some sense of morality. Even in the darkest, deepest jungles, people who have never been exposed to the divine law of God or scripture still have some type of moral code.

2. Positive Enactments

Positive enactments are the expression of God's will in published, written ordinance. This is what contained in scripture. There are different expressions of God's will for different ages or dispensations. Nevertheless, every age has a published ordinance from God.

Positive enactments are precepts expressed in three major categories:

First, there are moral precepts, such as the Ten Commandments and the Sermon on the Mount. **Second**, there are ceremonial precepts, such as the sacrificial system of the Law of Moses. **Third**, there are rules concerning the proper use of the spiritual gifts in the law of the Messiah.[8]

The Purpose of the Law of God

First and foremost, the law of God, regardless of which law or dispensation, was never to be a means of earning salvation (Rom. 3:20, 8:3; Gal. 3:21, NKJV).

Second, the purpose of the law of God was to intensify man's knowledge of sin (Rom. 3:19–20, 5:13, 20; 1 Cor. 15:56; Gal. 3:19, NKJV).

Third, the purpose of the law of God was to reveal the holiness of God (Rom. 7:12, NKJV).

Fourth, while the purpose of the law of God was not a means of salvation, it was to lead man to the means of salvation, which is saving faith (Gal. 3:24, NKJV).

Fifth, the purpose of the law of God is to provide the rule of life for the believer. Once a person is saved, some of the questions they may ask are "How then shall I live?" "What does God expect of the believers?"

For the believer in the Old Testament, the rule of life is the Law of Moses. For the believer now, the rule of life is the law of the Messiah. But regardless of which law it was—the law of the Abrahamic covenant, the law of Mosaic covenant, the law of the Messiah, and the law of God—it was never to attain salvation. Rather, it was to provide a rule of life for the believer.[8]

The Believer and the Law of God

Regarding the believer and the law of God, there are two important points to keep in mind. They are simple, yet people are very confused about these things and do not know which law to follow. Sometimes we disobey commandments applicable to us and obey commandments that are not. The first point is that believers today are not under the Law of Moses; the Law of Moses was given to the Jews. This means that not even 1 of the 613 commandments is applicable to the believers today. This is taught in Romans 6:14–15, 7:6; Galatians 5:18, and Hebrews 7:18–19 (NKJV).[8]

The second point concerning the believers of the law of God is that believers are under the law of the Messiah. Just as the Law of Moses contained many commandments, the laws of the Messiah are the same as those founding the Law of Moses, but many others are different. Therefore, we should clearly understand that believers are not under the Law of Moses today; we have no obligation to obey any of the 613 commandments of the Law of Moses.

However, believers today have every obligation to obey all the commandments of the law of the Messiah. This is taught in Romans 8:4, 1 Corinthians 9:21, and Galatians 5:18, 6:2 (NKJV). Disobeying a commandment of the law of the Messiah, either passively or actively, is a sin against God. (9)

As I sought for a prayer to end this chapter, I went to the Psalm of David, when Nathan the prophet came unto him after he had gone into Bathsheba. Many of us may never arrange the death of another human being as David did, but the Word of God said we all have sinned and have come short of the glory of God. We all can relate to David through this prayer.

Maurine McFarlane

Prayer of David

Psalm 51:1–19 (NKJV)

Have mercy upon me, O God, according to thy

lovingkindness: according unto the multitude

of thy tender mercies blot out my transgressions.

Wash me thoroughly from mine iniquity, and cleanse me from my sin.

For I acknowledge my transgressions: and my sin is ever before me.

Against thee, thee only, have I sinned, and done this evil in thy sight:

that thou mightiest be justified when thou speakest, and be clear when thou judgest.

Behold, I was shapen in iniquity; and in sin did my mother conceives me.

Behold, thou desirest truth in the inward parts: and in the
hidden part thou shalt make me to know wisdom.

Purge me with hyssop, and I shall be clean: wash me, and I shall be whiter than snow.

Make me to hear joy and gladness; that the bones which thou hast broken may rejoice.

Hide thy face from my sins and blot out all mine iniquities.

Create in me a clean heart, O God; and renew a right spirit within me.

Cast me not away from thy presence; and take not thy holy spirit from me.

Restore unto me the joy of thy salvation; and uphold me with thy free spirit.

Then will I teach transgressors thy ways; and sinners shall be converted unto thee.

Deliver me from bloodguiltiness, O God, thou God of my salvation: and my tongue shall sing aloud of thy righteousness.

O Lord open thou my lips; and my mouth shall shew forth thy praise.

For thou desirest not sacrifice; else would I give it: thou delightest not in burnt offering.

The sacrifices of God are a broken spirit: a broken and a contrite heart, O God,

thou wilt not despise.

Do good in thy good pleasure unto Zion: build thou the walls of Jerusalem.

Then shalt thou be pleased with the sacrifices of righteousness, with burnt offering and whole burnt offering: then shall they offer bullocks upon thine altar.

ENDNOTES:

1   Dr. Arnold G. Fruchtenbaum, "The Explanation of Sin," *What the Bible Teaches Concerning Sin: A Messianic Bible Study* (San Antonio, Texas: Ariel Ministries Press), 8, https://ariel.org.nz/wp-content/uploads/2018/08/23-What-bible-teaches-about-sin-mbs095m.pdf.

2   Fruchtenbaum, "The Definition and Meaning of Sin," *What the Bible Teaches Concerning Sin: A Messianic Bible Study*, 9.

3   Fruchtenbaum, "The Essential Nature of Sin," *What the Bible Teaches Concerning Sin: A Messianic Bible Study*, 9.

4   Fruchtenbaum, "The Transmission of the Sin-Nature," *What the Bible Teaches Concerning Sin: A Messianic Bible Study*, 13.

5   Fruchtenbaum, "The Penalty for the Sin-Nature," *What the Bible Teaches Concerning Sin: A Messianic Bible Study*, 13.

6   Fruchtenbaum, "The Penalty for Personal Sin," *What the Bible Teaches Concerning Sin: A Messianic Bible Study*, 16.

7   Fruchtenbaum, "Transmission of Personal Sin," *What the Bible Teaches Concerning Sin: A Messianic Bible Study*, 17.

8   Fruchtenbaum, "The Nature of the Law," *What the Bible Teaches Concerning Sin: A Messianic Bible Study*.

CHAPTER SIX

THE REMEDY FOR PERSONAL SIN

W hen we think of remedies, we normally think of something to make whatever illness or sickness we have better, but there is one sickness we all share for which there is no natural remedy. *That sickness is the disease of sin.* While some may choose to ignore sin in their own lives and in our world today, they are unable to explain why things are the way they are if the sickness of sin is overlooked. The thing about this disease, which already leads all people to death, is that *if left untreated, it can also lead to eternal death and separation from God.* No homemade, natural remedies work with this deadly disease. Only God has the remedy for sin, a supernatural remedy.

I can try and justify my sins by saying they are not as bad as the other person's sins; they are more "respectable." REALLY? Are some sins "respectable"? Of course they are not. God hates every sin, and all of them both big and small nailed our Lord to the cross and grieve the Holy Spirit that lives within. Today's culture has pretty much denied the existence of sin, preferring medical and psychiatric words to describe the bad things we do. While the church has not gone as far as the world, she is moving in the same direction, calling sin by new names and making it less serious than it really is. Sin is real, it is also malignant, and that means dangerous, and if unchecked, it will spread all over the soul and kill us. The first tumor of sin is seldom a big one; often it is a "respectable" sin.

Remedy for Personal Sin

Concerning the remedy for personal sin, here are two facets involved: forgiveness and justification. *The first remedy* for personal sin is forgiveness. When a person receives Jesus as Savior, he is forgiven of his sins. This means that God removes the sins of the one who has exercised faith in the substitutionary death, burial, and resurrection of the Messiah. The first penalty, guilt, is removed by forgiveness.

The second remedy for personal sin is justification, which means "to be declared righteous." The one who believes in the Lord Jesus the Messiah is declared to be righteous. The result of the remedy for personal sin is personal salvation. God's remedy was foretold as the one whom he would send, the one who would crush the head of the serpent (Gen. 3:15, NKJV). God also taught Adam and Eve that sin was not something for which they could find their own remedy. Fig leaf coverings were inadequate.

To deal with sin, the remedy must come from God. God himself covered their uncomfortable nakedness; the symbol of *God's remedy for sin was to do away with sin at its source, the devil.* God has the remedy for sin, and it centers in his Son Jesus Christ, a remedy received by faith. Christ is the fulfillment of what God promised our first parents in Eden that the one born of the woman would crush the head of the serpent, the devil, and destroy its power. *God's remedy for sin is Jesus Christ*, and God's remedy takes us back to what happened in that desert so long ago.

In church one day, I heard the words of our Lord himself say, "As Moses lifted up the serpent in the wilderness, even so must the Son of Man be lifted up that everyone who believes in Him may have eternal life." On the cross at Calvary, God was working out his divine remedy, for sin has his only Son paid the penalty for our sin.

Yes, Jesus died in our place, paying the price for our rebellion, our complaining, our whining, our rationalizations for sin, our faithlessness, our doubts, and our unbelief. By his death and resurrection, Jesus has crushed the head of the serpent and destroyed Satan's power! God's remedy for sin is forgiveness and eternal life offered to all who will receive Christ as their Savior! Only faith in Jesus Christ as Savior and his death on the cross for us saves us! "But God, being rich in mercy, because of the great love with which He loved us, even when we were dead in our trespasses, made us alive together with Christ by grace you have been saved" (Eph. 2:4, NKJV).

Yes, God's grace has given us the one and only complete remedy for sin, Jesus Christ! Let us not grow weary and impatient as we wander in this wilderness called earth before God takes us to the Promised Land of heaven. *God provides all we need for our daily lives in this sin-filled world, and God has provided the remedy for sin, his Son, Jesus Christ.* During this wilderness, God has set up a cross upon which the perfect sacrifice for sin has been offered once and for all. Sin and death have been completely conquered! Let us keep our eyes firmly fixed upon Jesus and so live today, tomorrow, and always.

Prayer as a Sinner

Dear God, I confess that I am a sinner in need of a Savior.

Thank you, Lord, for sending your Son, Jesus Christ,

to the earth to die for my sin

through the shedding of his blood that I may have eternal life.

I believe he died and rose on the third day and ascended to heaven,

where he sits at the right hand of the Father, and he will

come again to judge the living and the dead.

I receive this gift of life you give so freely to me.

Thank you for forgiving me of my sins and cleansing me of my iniquities.

In Jesus's name,

Amen.

CHAPTER SEVEN

SOLITUDE WITH GOD

Before you begin asking God for things, you may want to get to know him first. Do you remember when you met the person you believed is the one for you? You would spend hours on the phone talking with that person. You want to hear their voice, to learn as much as you can about them. You could not wait to see that person. The more you learned about that person, the more connected you are to that individual. You know when they are upset with you or when you do something that pleased them. This is how we define intimate relationship, a relation that is built overtime, marked by close acquaintance, association, or familiarity. Someone to whom private matters are confided, having a mutual interest or affections of established friendship. This is how it must be when developing a relationship with God, spending much time in solitude with God, reading his word. Through the Word of God, you will get to know him personally for yourself, not someone else's idea of who God is.

Real intimacy makes us feel alive, like we have been found, as if someone finally took the time to peer into the depths of our soul and really see us there. Until then, until we experience true intimacy, we will feel passed over and ignored, like someone is looking right through us. When God gets us alone through sufferings, heartbreaks, disappointments, sicknesses, temptations, and broken friendships, and we are totally speechless, unable to ask any questions, then he begins to teach us. Jesus does not take us aside and explains things to us all the time. He explains things to us as we are able to understand them. "When they were alone, He explained all things to His disciples" (Mark 4:34, NKJV).

As you journey with God, the only thing he intends to be clear is the way he deals with your soul. The lives of others are examples to us, but God requires us to examine our own soul. It is a slow work, so slow that it takes God all of time and eternity to make a man or woman conform to his purpose. God can only use us after we allow him to show us the deep, hidden areas of our own character. Oswald Chambers said, "It is astounding how ignorant we are about ourselves. We do not recognize the envy, laziness, or pride within us when we see it." But Jesus will reveal to us everything we have held within ourselves before his grace began to work. Oswald asked the question, "How many of us have learned to look inwardly with courage?" He insists that we must get rid of the idea that we understand ourselves.

This is the last bit of pride to go. The only one who understands us is God. The greatest curse of our spiritual life is pride. Whenever there is any element of pride or conceit remaining, Jesus cannot teach us anything. He will allow us to experience heartbreak or the disappointment we feel when our intellectual pride is wounded. He will reveal numerous misplaced affections or desires above him, things over which we never thought he would have to get us alone about. Many things are shown to us, often without effect, but when God gets us alone over them, they will be clear.[1]

We think we understand another person's struggle until God reveals the same shortcomings in our lives. There are vast areas of stubbornness and ignorance the Holy Spirit will reveal in each of us alone. Are you alone with him now? Or are you more concerned with your own ideas and friendship than you are about the concerns of Jesus? Jesus cannot teach us anything until we quiet all our intellectual questions and get alone with him. Solitude teaches us that we do not need other people in the way that we usually think we need them. It teaches us that our value is not determined by our usefulness to others. Solitude teaches us to hear the voice of God since we are cut off from the hundreds of other voices that call out to us from our usual company. Solitude forces us to face despair, yet it provides the only opportunity to discover the amazing power of God's presence.

Too often we run from our loneliness. I am sensitive to the dark power of despair and loneliness; the pain defies explanation. However, I have discovered that it is often during such experiences that God's presence is most powerfully felt. It is only here that I truly comprehend the words of Jesus, "I am with you always, even to the end of the age" (Matt. 28:20, NKJV).[1]

Solitude and silence combined with a mind that is actively waiting on God will enable us to view life as God reveals it to us. We will consider our actions and the motives behind them. We will consider the actions of others and allow God to season our response with compassion and forgiveness because we first recognize the compassion and forgiveness God has shown to us. In solitude, we discover that our infinitely empty lives can only find fulfillment in an infinite God. So in solitude, we seek him and find him! The most amazing thing occurs when our emptiness has been replaced by the fullness of his presence. We begin to view all other parts of life in a new way. God removes the "continual lust for more" (Eph. 4:19, NKJV) that results from a life apart from him and replaces it with contentment and ridiculous generosity.[2]

Well, how do you do it? How does a person go about putting these principles into practice? There are many ways. Allow me to suggest the following principles and practices that work in my life. Solitude with God may require time and space. Make a place where your quiet time can occur uninterrupted, for example, a library, a room in your home, a room in a church, or someplace else where you will not be interrupted. I created an altar in my living room for my quiet time with God. You can make a spare room in your house into a sanctuary. Create a regular, nonnegotiable place in your schedule that is solely for being alone and still before God.

In the beginning of my relationship with God, I decided that if I was going to get to know him, I needed to dedicate a certain amount of time with him. I like to start my day in the presence of God. I start my day between 3:30–4:00 a.m., making sure that no one else in the house is awake. I devote time to him again just before I go to bed between 10:00–11:00 p.m. If you have large blocks of time where you are alone (at home, in the car), leave the television, radio, and so on off and focus your thoughts on scriptures and in prayer. We who know how to worry also know how to meditate. It is just a matter of what our minds dwell on.

Carve out three or four days where you can be completely alone. There are many retreat centers designed specifically for such a purpose. When you develop a habit of solitude and silence, you will be able to take them with you wherever you go, especially in the hectic places of your life. Look for the short times each day where you can find solitude and silence. Use those times to focus your attention on seeking God's presence.

- The quiet morning moments before you get out of bed
- The quiet after the children have gone to school
- The short drive to work (leave the radio off)
- The traffic jams on the way to work
- The moments you see a beautiful blue sky or green fields or imposing mountains. Let them direct your thoughts on the creator.

Solitude always requires attention. In a world of troubles and uncertainty, it can be challenging to stay focused, but you must press yourselves. Solitude without engaging the mind will put you to sleep. The point of your time in solitude and silence is to do nothing, and do not try to make anything happen. "In solitude and silence, you're learning to stop doing, stop producing, stop pleasing people, stop entertaining yourself, stop obsessing, stop doing anything except to *simply be your naked self before God and be found by him*."[3]

MAURINE McFARLANE

Prayer for Solitude

My Lord and my God, you are my Savior.

I desire to know more of you, Lord. Teach me to be still

that I may see your salvation.

Teach me to listen that I may hear your quiet voice.

Teach me to discern your voice from mine, to perceive

the Father within myself.

Teach me to welcome solitary moments, to enjoy

the solitude within myself,

while listening to your inspirations.

Teach me to practice your patience and love for others.

In Jesus's name, I pray.

Amen.

ENDNOTES:

1   Oswald Chambers, *My Utmost for His Highest* (Oswald Chambers Publications, 1992).
2   Gordon MacDonald, "Solitude and Silence," *Renewing Your Spiritual Passion* (Edinburg: Thomas Nelson Inc., 1997).
3   Bill Gaultier, "Solitude and Silence," *Soul Shepherding*, 2005, 2012, https://www.soulshepherding.org/solitude-and-silence.

CHAPTER EIGHT

THE REALITY OF OUR RIGHTEOUSNESS

What does it mean to be righteous? After so many years in my relationship with God, and in the process of writing my second book, I am just beginning to learn what that really means. I wonder why it took GOD so long to reveal the reality of his righteousness to me. I have been blinded by religion on what it means to be righteous. As a result, I spend many years going around in circles and never coming into the fullness of who I am in Christ until now. No wonder he insisted on me writing this book, *Fighting for My Destiny: How I Learned to Pray to Get What I Need*. If I am going to see the vision, my purpose, and the promises of God manifest in my life, I first need to understand what Jesus Christ did for me on the cross. I needed to understand the significance of the sacrifice of what God did for me, not just knowing he died for my sins but what happened after that.

The Bible says, "My people are destroyed for lack of knowledge" (Hosea 4:6, NKJV). I believe this scripture is saying we have the Bible, which is the Word of God, and there in is all the information one needs for instruction in righteousness and holy living. It is one thing to know your Bible, but it is another thing to KNOW the God of the Bible. When Jesus had gone forty days in the desert fasting and praying, Jesus was hungry and at a weak point. One translation says, "He was faint with hunger." The devil, the tempter came to him. The question I put to you, dear friends, is this: *When does the devil tempt you the most?* It is usually at your weakest moment. *How did Jesus handle this moment?* He brought God into it. He quoted the Bible, God's Word. Each time the devil tried to trap Jesus, Jesus would respond, "It is written!" Many of us are also robbed of blessings that the Bible tells us are ours in Christ Jesus. But because we do not know it, we never truly live in them.

Before I experienced God's righteousness by faith, I prayed sometimes for two hours, sometimes more every day. I also read my Bible every day. I went to church sometimes twice a week, and I still had a sin consciousness. I still felt weak. I was still very much aware of my sin and my failures. But when I had my eyes unveiled, I literally became a new person. Within a short time, I went from a miserable Romans 7 experience into the glorious liberation of a child of God.

I was a baby when I found this out. I was a Christian, but I began to grow, and I began to walk in the things of God. I began to believe the Word of God in ways I never did before. How can I stay in fear and darkness when he said, "He hath delivered us from the power of darkness, and hath translated us into the kingdom of his dear Son" (Col. 1:13, KJV)?

The Bible clearly states that human beings cannot achieve righteousness through their own efforts. Righteousness is a gift; we cannot work for it. "Therefore no one will be declared righteous in God's sight by the works of the law; rather, through the law we become conscious of our sin" (Rom. 3:20, NIV). We receive righteousness through faith in Jesus Christ as Savior. Christ, the sinless Son of God, took humanity's sin upon himself and became the willing, perfect sacrifice, suffering the punishment mankind deserved. God the Father accepted Jesus's sacrifice, through which human beings can become justified.

In turn, we receive righteousness from Christ. This doctrine is called imputation. When Jesus entered the world, things changed. His crucifixion and resurrection satisfied God's justice. Christ's shed blood covers our sins. No more sacrifices or works are required. The apostle Paul explains how we receive righteousness through Christ in the book of Romans. Salvation through this crediting of righteousness is a gift, which is the doctrine of grace. Salvation by grace through faith in Jesus is the essence of Christianity. No other religion offers grace. They all require some type of works on behalf of the participant. Christ's perfect righteousness is applied to imperfect humans.

The Bible tells us that none of us are righteous in and of ourselves (Ps. 14:1–3, NLT). There is nothing we can do to make ourselves righteous, but God himself has provided us with the righteousness we need. Romans 1:17 (NLT) states, "The good news tells us how God makes us right in his sight. This is accomplished from start to finish by faith. As the scripture says, 'It is through faith that a righteous person has life.'"

What happens when we believe? We are born again, then the Holy Spirit of God baptizes us. The purpose of the Holy Spirit is to arrange the furniture in our lives so we can be productive. A visiting pastor who spoke at my church taught us the benefits of this gift. It is so profound and brings a greater understanding to me about my salvation I thought it was necessary to share it with you. *What do we get from the GIFT of Salvation?* First, according to 2 Corinthians 1:20 (NKJV), "All of God's promises are 'Yes,' and in him Amen, unto the glory of God by us.' We receive the gift of salvation by grace through faith.

The five promises that come with the gift of salvation are the following:

1. **Forgiveness:** Ephesians 1:7 (NKJV) says, "In Him we have redemption through His blood, the forgiveness of sins, according to the riches of His grace." We are forgiven of all our sins, past, present, and the future.
2. **Deliverance:** Forgiveness and deliverance go hand in hand from every sting of the enemy. Ephesians 2:3–5 (NKJV) says that among whom also we all had our conversation in times past in the lust of our flesh, fulfilling the desires of the flesh and of the mind; and whereby nature the children of wrath, even as others. But God, who is rich in mercy, for

His great love wherewith He loved us. Even when we were dead in sins, hath quickened us together with Christ, (by grace we are saved).

3. **Healing:** Healing is the children's bread (Matt. 15:26–28; Isa. 53:5, NKJV). He was wounded for our transgressions, he was bruised for our iniquities, the chastisement of our peace was upon him, and with his stripes, we are healed. Healing belongs to us as a child of God.

4. **Baptism of the Holy Spirit:** The Holy Spirit is the deity of God who continues to apply the power of the atonement by the cross of Christ in our lives. This is where we get the gifts of the Spirit. The gifts are for the ministry to the unsaved. There is a security in Christ Jesus if we have faith.

5. **Prosperity:** Prosperity is the will of God for us, but it is more than finance; it is prosperity in all areas of our lives.

Having faith in Christ removes our sin and activates the righteousness of God and applies it to our lives. It is not our righteousness but his. *So why do we trust our feelings more than we trust the Word of God?* Our sin conscious, which is based on how we feel, is a state of being where we feel separated from God. We do not sense our oneness with God, but we are very aware of our sin. We are very aware of our lack; we are very aware of our inability to do that which we want to do. Sin consciousness is that state where we can want with all our heart to please God, and yet we find within our members that sin consciousness. The sense of being separated, the sense of failure, and the sense of fear. "Oh, I would love to be able to pray with my coworkers, but I feel so inferior." That is sin consciousness, and that will rob us and steal from us everything that God wants us to have.

Sin consciousness destroys faith. How can we have faith to believe for anything from God if we feel inferior and if we are so aware of our sin and our shortcomings? This creates an inferiority complex in us. "I would love to be able to stand up for the least of these, but I can't." "I wish I had the boldness to share the gospel with people, but I can't." "I wish I could be a better person, but I can't." This is sin consciousness.

Let us look at Ephesians 2:12 (NKJV). This is the man who has a sin consciousness because of his separation from God. Paul says to the Ephesians, "That at that time ye were without Christ, being aliens from the commonwealth of Israel, and strangers from the covenants of promise, having no hope, and without God in the world." Now if you are in this condition today, you certainly do have a sin consciousness.

If we do not have Christ, we have no hope. Jesus said to the Pharisees, "You are of your father the devil." We are not the Jews, God's people. But Jesus said, "You are of your father the devil," *because words express what we are.*

Our Father is the source of our lives, we receive life from our Father. If we are speaking words of failure and defeat, words of our inabilities, or words of our inferiorities, we are identifying with the ungodly part of our nature and speaking from our carnal nature. Out of the abundance of the heart, the mouth speaks. Romans 8:14–15 (NKJV) said, for as many as are led by the Spirit of God, they are the sons of God. For we have not received the spirit of bondage again to fear, but we have received the Spirit of adoption, whereby we cry, Abba, Father. The Spirit of God bears witness with our spirit, that we are the children of God. As children of God walking in righteousness through Christ, then we have the right to a healthy, prosperous, peaceful, joyous, and victorious life, a holy life, which is the fruit of our righteousness.

We Have a New Nature

What does that mean? What is the distinction between the "old man" and the "new man" ("man" being a reference to humanity, not a specific gender) and its relevant outworking in the life of the Christian? One way to view "nature" is to understand it as a "capacity" within a believer. Thus, the old man is interpreted as the former way of life, that of an unbeliever. In this sense, the Christian has two competing capacities within, the old capacity to sin and the new capacity to resist sinning. The unbeliever has no such competition within; he does not have the capacity for godliness because he has only the sin nature. That is not to say he cannot do "good works," but his motivation for those works is always tainted by his sinfulness. In addition, he cannot resist sinning because he does not have the capacity to not sin. The believer, on the other hand, has the capacity for godliness because the Spirit of God lives within him. He still has the capacity for sin as well, but he now has the ability to resist sin and, more importantly, the desire to resist and to live a godly life.

When Christ was crucified, the old man was crucified with him, resulting in the Christian no longer being a slave to sin (Rom. 6:6, ASV). We "have been set free from sin and have become slaves to righteousness" (Rom. 6:18, ASV). At the moment of conversion, the Christian receives a new nature. It is instantaneous. Sanctification, on the other hand, is the process by which God develops our new nature, enabling us to grow into more holiness through time. This is a continuous process with many victories and defeats as the new nature battles with the "tent" in which it resides the old man, old nature, the flesh.

The same thought is captured in Paul's testimony: "I have been crucified with Christ and I no longer live, but Christ lives in me. The life I live in the body, I live by faith in the Son of God, who loved me, and gave Himself for me" (Gal. 2:20, ASV). Paul says I died, but I live, obviously a new and different person. We as Christians have a new identity, and it comes from who we are in Christ, not who we were in Adam.

A New Heart and a New Spirit

One of the greatest prophecies concerning our salvation is given in Ezekiel 36:26: "I will give you a new heart and put a new spirit within you; I will remove from you a heart of stone and give you a heart of flesh." Jesus came that we might have life, and the believer receives that spiritual life at the moment of salvation. "Yet to all who received Him, to those who believed in His name, He gave the right to become children of God" (John 1:12, ASV). The moment you were grafted into the vine, you were sanctified or set apart as a child of God. "You are already clean" (John 15:3, ASV), and you shall continue to be sanctified as he prunes you so that you may grow and bear fruit. You are now alive in Christ, which is the foundation and source for the spiritual growth. In fact, the believer is described as a new creation with a new life that has new desires and a new direction.

Saved and Sanctified by Faith

Again we need to understand that this is a reality that has already taken place. Paul says, "Our old self was crucified" (past tense). We try and try to put the old man to death, and we cannot do it. *Why not?* Because he is already dead! We cannot do for ourselves what Christ has already done for us. For a long time, I was not living the abundant life, and many Christians are not living the abundant life today. Like me, they incorrectly reason, "What experience has to happen in order for this to be true?" The only thing that had to happen for that to be true happened over two thousand years ago, and the only way you or I can enter this experience is by faith. We must learn to accept what God says is true and live accordingly by faith. *If we try to make what God says true by our experiences, we will never get there.*

Paul points out the futility of that thinking in Galatians 3:2 (ASV): "I would like to learn just one thing from you. Did you receive the Spirit by observing the law, or by believing what you heard? Are you so foolish? After beginning with the Spirit, are you now trying to attain your goal by human effort?" We are saved by faith, and we walk or live by faith. We have been sanctified by faith, and we are being sanctified by faith and by faith alone. We are neither saved nor sanctified by how we behave but by how we believe. God satisfies the emptiness in us by taking out of us that old nature.

Do you know that if you have the devil in you and God in you at the same time, you have two fathers? Would God do that kind of a work? How could you ever have any confidence in God with that mentality? That is not the word. That is religion; that is philosophy. You know what philosophy is? It is reasoning. Philosophy will give you all the reasons that you need to justify your condition. "I'm just human. What do you think I am, God?" If you could understand what God has given you—his life, his character, his nature. He has given us a new heart and put his

Spirit in us, and we are now as he is in this world. It is time that the church realizes that we are not mere humans. *What did we receive when we received God's nature?*

Authority in the Spirit

Since we are identified with Christ in his death and resurrection, we have become a new person and part of the new humanity. In this change, we have come under a new power of dominion in our life. Nowhere is this expressed more clearly than in Romans 6:5–7 (ASV): "If we have been united with Him…in His death, we will certainly also be united with Him in His resurrection. For we know that our old self was crucified with Him so that the body of sin might be done away with, that we should no longer be slaves to sin, because anyone who has died has been freed from sin."

"Old self" in this passage is literally "old man." The "old man" in relation to the believer has been crucified in Christ, and he has put on the "new man" (Col. 3:10, ASV). He gave them authority, even in the Old Testament. We've lost some of the understanding of the word because of the translation in the King James, but the word says, "If you abide in me and my words abide in you, you may ask what you will" (John 15:7, ASV). The word "ask" if you look up the root word means "to demand." Do you know you do not have to ask the Father for anything? Did Jesus? No! He knew the will of the Father, and he just spoke. Jesus said, "Hither to, you've asked nothing. You ask in My name, and I will give it to you. My Father will give to you." It is time for us as Christians to stand up and demand our rights according to the scriptures. "I am the righteousness of God in Christ and I command this sin consciousness to leave me."[1]

If the church takes this word, they will find their freedom. All the hordes of darkness could not keep Jesus in the pits of hell. He arose from the grave, stripped off principalities and powers, made a show of them openly, triumphing over them at the cross, and you can do the same thing. Not so that you can look at him as some superhuman. Do not misunderstand me, but the word says he was the firstborn, He was the firstborn of the new creation. *He became the first born among many brethren. Where has the church been?* In religion, trying to appease God through works.

I will tell you, I did it! For years, I prayed every day, hours sometimes. I used to cry. "God, am I ever going to win?" But when the blinders came off, what liberty I found. God just said something simple to me one day. He said, "Why are you trying so hard to become something that I've already made you to be? Why are you trying so hard? Just believe me, Maurine. Read my word and just believe me." I was so excited that I finally got it, and I believed it because I did it. I started to call my friends; they needed to know what I have just been revealed to me. Behold in the Word of God that which God says that you are. Think about it. Meditate on it.

Speak it day and night, and it will be yours. You see, it does not come by works of righteousness that we have done.

We Are More Than Just Human

In Genesis 2:7 (NASB), the Bible says, "The Lord God Formed man of dust from the ground, and breathed into his nostrils the breath of life, and man became a living being." When God breathed into us, we became an extension of him. Before the fall of man, we were given authority of the earth. "God formed every beast of the field and very bird of the sky and brought them to the man to see what he would call them; and whatever the man called a living creature that was its name" (Gen. 2:19, NASB).

God armed humanity with authority over all the creatures and earth itself. God gave mankind dominion over the earth to rule it. Earth still belonged to God, but he gave it over to men to rule over it. God, the ultimate ruler and authority of all things, gave humanity its own little corner of creation to rule over. Genesis 1:26–27 says, "Then God said, 'Let us make man in our image, in our likeness, and let them rule over the fish of the sea and the birds of the air, over the livestock, over all the earth, and over all the creatures that move along the ground.'"

When God establishes an issue, it is established. Just as creation is bound to follow the natural laws established by God, God follows his own laws. Since God is ultimately righteous, God's Word is ultimately true. God cannot go back on his word because to deny his word would be to deny his authority, which establishes his word as truth.[1]

Because of Adam's sin, God turned away from Adam and all of humanity, after him because God's kingdom only includes those who serve him. The earth itself was cut off from God because God had given humanity authority over it. Adam had cut himself off from God and rebelled against God's authority over humanity by disobeying God's one law for mankind. Follow the chain of events: God gives authority over the earth to humanity. Humanity is cut off from God because of sin. The earth is cursed, separated from God, because humanity has authority over it, and humanity is separated from God by spiritual death.

Since God gave legal authority over earth to humanity, God must honor his word. Having given man authority over the earth, God no longer has legitimate right to operate directly in the earth. God must find humans with authority in the earth who are willing to work with God to accomplish his plans for the redemption of humanity.

Jesus came with the authority of God, although he did not use that authority except under God's direction. He gave his authority to his followers while he was on earth (Luke 9:1, John 14:12, NASB). The Great Commission, in fact, was given through Jesus's authority (Matt. 28:18, NASB). It is through Jesus's death that man is restored as second under God (1 Cor. 15:45–47, NASB). The result of this is that Christians have authority over angels, including demons, because Jesus gave us that authority. He delegated his authority to us to use according to his will on earth.

We are, in fact, God's sons and daughters. So we exercise spiritual authority in God's name, and demons must obey us, just as they did Jesus. However, although the authority has been given to us, the power comes from God. If we misuse our authority, God may not exercise his power. Thus, it is important for us to spend time with God, just as Jesus did, to figure out what his will is. It is only by knowing God's will that we can confidently exercise our authority. It is also important to recognize some limits to our authority. We are to only use it in love, as a servant, to help others. It is not to be used for building our power or reputation. We need to be humble because the Almighty God is trusting us with his authority. We need to examine whether our exercise of authority results in godly fruit. We must use our authority in obedience; we cannot command God, just name it and claim it or expect God to bless the plans we made without asking him. We should also recognize that even though we have God's authority, and we may know his overall will, this may not be the time when God wants to accomplish his will. And we need to remember that it is not our power that is doing this, nor are we indispensable to God.

The prayer of a righteous person is powerful and effective (James 5:16, NASB). The Bible has a lot to say about prayer; after all, it is the way we communicate with our Lord. And all of it promises that God hears and answers prayers, especially those offered by two or more in agreement (Matt. 18:19, NASB). The Lord personally promised his disciples that he will do whatever we ask in his name so that the Son may bring glory to the Father (John 14:13, 15:7, 15:16, NASB).

Prayer of the Righteous Person

Father, I give you thanks.

I give you praise and glory. I give you honor.

I also come humbly before you, admitting my great need for you.

Not simply a partial need, Lord, but a comprehensive,

deep, constant, and daily need.

Thank you that you give grace to the humble.

And so I humble myself before you and ask that

you would pour out your grace in

mighty measures today.

Graciously speaking to me.

Graciously touching my heart.

Graciously working in me to will and to do

according to your good pleasure.

And graciously transforming my life to the image of Jesus Christ.

By your Holy Spirit, unfold your word and make it alive to me.

And. Lord, I confess that I can only live by every

word that proceeds from your mouth.

So speak to me. I am ready to hear what you have to say.

In Jesus's name,

Amen.

ENDNOTE

1   Bob Hoekstra, "The Holy Spirit and the Grace of God," *Blue Letter Bible*, accessed July 11, 2013, https://www.blueletterbible. org/Comm/hoekstrabob/grace/grace04.cfm.

CHAPTER NINE

THE WORD OF GOD

What is the Word of God? According to 2 Timothy 3:16 (AMP), scripture is the inspired Word of God. "All scripture is given by inspiration of God." The word is given to us for doctrine, reproof, instruction, inspiration, and guidance. Think of a car. The person or company that creates that car knows every detail of that car, how many miles you need to drive it before you have to change the oil or have it tuned up. What the nuts and bolts are, where each part must fit to run properly, what type of gasoline to put in the car for maximum efficiencies. There are many things about that car the person purchasing the car needs to know; therefore, you get a book of instruction and guidance with you when purchase your new car.

The same is true for us; the Bible is our book of instructions for us on how to live, love, share, and communicate with God. "Your word is a lamp to my feet and a light to my path" (Ps. 19:105, AMP). God's Word, the Holy Bible, illuminates; it reveals to us the good and the bad, the wise and the unwise. It is the ultimate tool in learning how to live the best possible life, free from the restraints, of stumbling in darkness. The Bible is a book so intensive that you will want to live inside the pages. Indeed it is a set of "Basic Instructions before Leaving Earth."

Now we are going to figure out why we have the Word of God. That the man of God tells us in his word. *Who is the man of God?* God tells us in his word that Moses was a man of God (Deut. 33:1, AMP), Samuel is called a man of God (1 Sam. 9), and Elijah was a man of God (1 Kings 17:18, AMP). There are several other references in the Old Testament that define "man of God" and refer to those who spoke for God. When you speak the accuracy of God's Word, you are a man (woman) of God, you are speaking for God, heralding forth his truths. God's purpose for the God-breathed scripture is that the one who speaks for God may be perfect. Perfect? Some may say we cannot be perfect; that is not what the word says. Some may try to make themselves perfect by works; that also is not what God is saying. The God-breathed word is given that we may be perfect.

Let us examine "perfect" to get its specific meaning. The word "perfect" here is *artios* in Greek. It is used only this once in the Bible. The Greek word *artios* means to be complete or fully equipped. It is used to describe a ship that is ready for a voyage; the ship has everything on it that it could possibly need. It is also used in the Greek to describe the ball and socket joint of the hip. It is perfect, *artios*. If anything is wrong with that joint or if there was something in that joint, it would be excruciatingly painful. The word perfect, *artios*, means to be fully equipped, perfect. The Word of God equips us fully. Our job is to read it, understand it accurately, and live it.[1]

We cannot live on bread alone; we need the Word of God. Our bodies are sustained because of the foods we eat, but what about our souls? Who we are? We need the word to feed our minds and our souls so that we may "prosper and be in health, even as our soul prosper" (2 John 2, NIV). The word feeds our soul so that we can renew our minds to the words that proceed out of the mouth of God and live abundantly like he has intended his people to do.

We have one fundamental spiritual problem: not believing the integrity of the Word of God, not believing that what God said he meant and what he meant he said. Most of us do not really believe that the Word of God is accurate, and we certainly do not believe and act on the promises that God has placed in his word. But when we do believe, we see prosperity and health and a dynamic spiritual walk with God. "Sanctify them by the truth; your word is truth" (John 17:17, NIV).

The Spirit of God uses the Word of God to make us like the Son of God. To become like Jesus, we must fill our lives with his word. The Bible says, "Through the Word we are put together and shaped up for the tasks God has for us" (2 Tim. 3:17, NIV). God's Word is unlike any other word. It is alive. Jesus said, "The words that I have spoken to you are spirit and are life" (John 6:63, NASB).[1]

Rick Warren, senior pastor and author of Saddleback Church in Lake Forest, California, said, "When God speaks, things change. Everything around us, all of creation exists because God said it. He spoke it all into existence. God's Word generates life, creates faith, produces change, frightens the Devil, causes miracles, heals hurts, builds character, transforms circumstances. The Word imparts joy, overcomes adversity, defeats temptation, infuses hope, releases power, cleanses our minds, brings things into being and guarantees our future forever! We cannot live without the Word of God! Never take it for granted. You should consider it as essential to your life as food." Job said, "I have treasured the words of his mouth more than my daily bread" (Job 23:12, NIV).

God's Word is the spiritual nourishment you must have to fulfill your purpose. Numbers 23:19 (NIV) states, "God is not human, that he should lie, not a human being, that he should change his mind. Does he speak and then not act? Does he promise and not fulfill?" Isaiah 55:10–13 (NIV) tells us he preached the Word of God because God's Word can bring about an alignment between the way God thinks and acts and the way people think and act. There is a strong emphasis in the scripture on the importance of our will being in alignment with the will of God.

Jesus made his greatest prayer when he sweat drops of blood and prayed, "Not my will, but your will be done." He taught his disciples to pray. "Your will be done in earth (or in their earthen vessels), as it is in heaven." "So is my word that goes out from my mouth: It will not return to me empty but will accomplish what I desire and achieve the purpose for which I sent it" (Isa. 55:11, NIV). "Through these he has given us his very great precious promises, so that through them we may participate in the divine nature and escape the corruption in the world caused by evil desires." The Word of God is so powerful it penetrates even to dividing soul and spirit, joints, and marrow, as stated in Hebrews 4:12 (NIV): "For the word of God is alive and active. Sharper than any double-edged sword, it penetrates even to dividing soul and spirit, joints and marrow; it judges the thoughts and attitudes of the heart." The all-powerful sword of the living God can cut through every defense our enemy can raise, down to the very division of bone and marrow.

When wielded by a servant of God, nothing can withstand its ability to cut straight to the core of a matter and uncover the truth. As soldiers in God's army, it is our responsibility and duty to use his word to discern the truth and then follow it. When God's Word shows us something wrong in ourselves, we can use this spiritual weapon to "surgically" remove the offending thoughts and actions (2 Cor. 10:4–5, NIV). Unlike all other pieces of the armor of God, which are solely defensive, the sword is uniquely suited for both defensive and offensive roles. A solid defense is invaluable, but the sword is the only way we can complete the work we have been given to do. Notice that Jesus Christ used the Bible to counter Satan's attacks (Matt. 4:4, 7, 10, NIV). We must also learn to live "by every word that proceeds from the mouth of God" (Matt. 4:4, NIV).

Nothing of a positive spiritual nature is affected apart from the Word of God. Neither psychology nor sociology, nor philosophy, nor any other "ology" or "ism" can or will do what God's Word alone can do. God's Word can deliver us from sin, impart wisdom, imbue with strength to do right, and a host of other blessed works. The Lord himself asks a rhetorical question: "Is not my word…like a hammer that breaketh the rock in pieces?" "Does not my word burn like fire?" says the Lord (Jer. 23:29, NIV). No force of man or nature can withstand the blows of the hammer of the word.

Though a heart be as hard as an adamant stone; though a soul has turned from God, lived in wickedness, persisted in rebellion for decades; though a man lies nearly lifeless on his deathbed, the Word of God can break through a hardened heart, save, and deliver. All opposition will finally succumb before the force of its inevitable truth. When a sinner rebels, the Word of God yields him into submission; when a saint repents, the Word of God gently hammers him into victory. What formidable opposition, what impossible situation, what daunting circumstance stands before you today? As you serve the Lord doing his will, all will fall before the hammer of his word.[1]

Some Christians think that because God is sovereign, it makes no difference what they speak out of their mouths. They believe that God will just do what he wants. But God qualifies his sovereignty. He tells us what he will and what he will not do. He has set up principles in the Kingdom of God. If we violate his principles, we suffer the consequences. The Word of God is to govern our thoughts, actions, and conversations.

The Kingdom of God operates on seeds and harvests. We know from the parable of the sower that the Word of God is the seed that the sower is to plant (Luke 8:11; Mark 4:20, NIV). Jesus said his words are alive. They contain life. The words in your Bible may look lifeless and powerless. Seeds do too. But they are not without life or power. In Mark 4:30–31 (NIV), Jesus explained that the Kingdom of God works like a seed. So if we are to understand God's kingdom and how he operates, we need to understand seeds.[2]

Seeds

* ### A seed is alive: it contains life.
  Your physical senses are incapable of judging whether a seed is alive or not. You cannot see, feel, hear, smell, or taste the life in a seed. There is only one way to prove a seed is alive—plant it.

* ### A seed does nothing until planted.
  Seeds do not grow sitting in a sack on your shelf. They must be planted in the proper place. If you desire the Word of God to produce in your life, you must decide to plant the Word in your heart and mind. The best way to plant the seed of God's Word in your life is by speaking the Word. Hearing others speak the Word is good—but will not produce as bountiful a harvest as speaking the Word yourself. Speaking God's Word with your mouth is essential. As we speak God's Word we are planting the seed in our heart for the harvest of results we desire.

  Romans 10:10 NKJ
  *   10 For with the heart one believes to righteousness, and with the mouth confession is made to salvation. Whatever you need to be saved or delivered from, confession (what you say) is essential.*

* ### A seed is much smaller than the plant it produces.
  The problem you face may seem huge. In comparison, a scripture may seem small. But when planted, that Word will grow in you and overcome the problem.

* ### A seed always produces after its kind.
  Galatians 6:7 NKJ
  *   7 Do not be deceived, God is not mocked; for whatever a man sows, that he will also reap. Whatever you need, or desire, find scriptures relating to that. Then*

plant those scriptures inside you in abundance. Those seeds will grow up and produce a harvest of what you need or desire.

* **A seed is powerful.**
  As a seed begins to grow, it will push up dirt, rocks, etc. Whatever the obstacles are, God's Word planted in your heart will push them out of the way.

* **A seed begins its growth in secret (underground).**
  The only way to tell if a seed is growing is to dig it up or wait for a plant to appear. If you dig up a seed, you may kill it.

* **A seed takes time to produce.**
  No one expects a seed to produce a harvest the same day that seed is planted. Sometimes the Word of God seems to spring up and bear fruit immediately. Yet, if we knew the details, we would understand that the fruit of the Word grew in that person's life over time.

* **A seed is persistent.**
  A seed never gives up but works day and night. Even when you are sleeping, the seed you have planted is working to grow and express itself in a fruitful harvest.

* **A seed is not affected by other seeds.**
  Whatever happens to other seeds does not make any difference to a specific seed. Each seed sticks to its own task. One wheat seed planted in a corn field will still produce wheat. Seed does not become discouraged, or quit, even if other seeds die.

* **A seed will stop growing without nourishment.**
  Planting a seed is not enough to assure a harvest. Seed must be protected and taken care of until harvest time. A seed which is dug, up, or not watered, will not produce.

* **More seeds planted produce a larger harvest.**
  2 Corinthians 9:6 NKJ

  6 But this I say: He who sows sparingly will also reap sparingly, and he who sows bountifully will also reap bountifully.

One of my students, Richard Riley, from the Transform Your Mind Interactive Learning Program, always sends me these wonderful words he receives from Kenneth Copeland Ministries to mediate on. They were inspiring to me, and I hope they will be for you also.

Feast on the Word

The Word of God is to your spirit as bread is to your body. When your body feeds on physical food, it produces a physical power called strength. When your spirit feeds on the spiritual food of the word, it produces spiritual power called faith. And just as you cannot eat one meal and then feed on the memory of it for several weeks, you cannot just remember what the word says and stay strong in faith. You must read it. Even if you have read it a hundred times, you need to read it again.

Think about this, we all know what lemons taste like from our memory. As you think about biting down on one, no doubt your mouth will begin to water right now. Now let me ask you this. Have you received any nourishment from that memory? No! Remembering the word is not enough. You must continually feed on what it says. Get it out and read it. Go to church and hear it preached. Yes, you can feed on the word that is on deposit in your spirit.

But remember this: You cannot get continued results if you do not spend time in prayer and in the Word of God, allowing the Spirit to nourish you daily. Do not try to live on the memory of your last spiritual meal. Replenish the force of faith within you. Feast on the Word of God today. Each morning before I get into the Word of God, I say this prayer.

Open Prayer

Heavenly Father, I come before you in the name of Jesus.

As I come into your word, I pray your word becomes life,

that it will fall on good ground and bear much fruit.

Through your word, O Lord, speak to your daughter,

make it plain, and make it clear,

in Jesus's name,

Amen.

ENDNOTE

1   Philip Owen, "The Word of God: A Hammer," *The Glory of God's Word*, July 11, 2013.

2   "God's Word Is a Seed," *Believers Church*, https://www.believers.org/believe/bel133.htm, July 11, 2013.

CHAPTER TEN

SURRENDER

When we think of surrendering, we automatically think we are giving up something, namely, rights to ourselves. The ability to let go and turn it over to someone else is not an easy thing for us to do as human, even if the one we are surrendering to is God. And when we do surrender, it is because we are looking for something from God in return.

In Mark 10:28, Peter began to say to him, "See, we have left and follow You." Jesus replies to this statement of Peter by saying that this surrender is "for My sake and the gospel's" (Mark 10:29, NKJV). It was not for what the disciples themselves would get out of it. Our motive for surrendering should not be for any personal gain at all. We have become so self-centered that we go to God only for something from him and not for God himself.

Where does Jesus figure in when we have concerns about our natural relationships? Most of us will desert him with this excuse: "I heard you call me, Lord, but my family needs me, or my business needs me, and I have my own interests. I just can't go any further." See Luke 14:26–33 (NKJV). Total surrender is a personal sovereign preference for Jesus Christ himself. Salvation does not mean merely deliverance from sin or the experience of personal holiness. The salvation that comes from God means being completely delivered from ourselves and being placed into perfect union with him. It means that the Spirit of God has brought us into intimate contact with the true person of God himself. And as we are caught up into total surrender to God, we will become thrilled with something infinitely greater than ourselves.

You will never know anything about surrender until you understand what John 3:16 (NKJV) means, that God completely and absolutely gave himself to us. In your surrender, you must give yourself to God in the same way he give himself for you—totally, unconditionally, and without reservation. The consequences and circumstances resulting from your surrender will never even enter your mind because your life will be totally consumed with him. True surrender will always go beyond natural devotion. Oswald Chambers writes, "If we will only give up, God will surrender Himself to embrace all those around us and will meet their needs, which were created by our surrender." Most of us have only a vision of what this really means but have never truly experienced it.

The Realism of Dismay to Surrender

In the beginning of my walk with Jesus Christ, I was sure I knew all there was to know about following him. It was a delight to forsake everything and follow Jesus in a fearless statement of love. But after eight years of sacrifice, I found out I was not quite so sure. I found out there are aspects of Jesus that will chill the most faithful follower's heart to its depth and make our spiritual life gasp for air. The longer the vision takes to manifest in my life, the greater the opportunity for the devil to convince me it will never come to pass.

The reason is, when we get a vision from God, and though it is real, it has not yet taken root in us. Satan comes and try to tempt us by making us believe the vision is not real and will not come to pass. We are inclined to believe there is no point to pursue. That is when doubting starts to creep into our heart, and our confidence in Jesus now becomes shaky. The confidence we once had by faith is replaced by doubt and uncertainties, questioning whether he is still a counselor or a friend. Before we know it, there is a distance between Jesus and us, and we can no longer be intimate with him. We have no idea where he is going, and the goal becomes strangely distant. Fear and anxiousness replace faith; it is in this valley many of us give up.

The lesson of dismay is an essential one we all must learn. The danger is that we tend to look back on our times of obedience and our past sacrifices to God in an effort to keep our enthusiasm for him. "Who among you fears the LORD and obeys his servant? If you are walking in darkness, without a ray of light, trust in the LORD and rely on your God. But watch out, you who live in your own light and warm yourselves by your own fires. This is the reward you will receive from me: You will soon fall in great torment" (Isa. 50:10–11, NKJV). It takes a while to learn these lessons, but when darkness comes, and the storms comes, we must be willing to admit, as we begin to examine what controls and dominates us, that we are the one responsible for submitting or yielding ourselves to whatever it might be.

Romans 6:6 (NKJV) says, "You are the one's slaves whom you obey." If we allow our selfishness or the right to ourselves to dominate, we are to be blame because somewhere in the past, we yield to ourselves. Likewise if we obey God, we do so because at some point in our life, we surrender to him. It is also important to realize that our carnal mind has not fully gone. We have no proof until we are tested. We should be careful not to deceive ourselves. When carnality is gone, we will know. It is the most real thing we can imagine, and God will see to it that we have a number of opportunities to prove to ourselves the miracle of his grace. At that point, we will be amazed at what God has done for us on the inside.

"I Want to...But"

Has God ever told you to do something that is a great test of your common sense? I mean totally going against everything you know as sensible. What do you do? Hold back, debate about it? If we get in the habit of doing something physical, we will do it every time we are tested until we break the habit through sheer determination. That is also what happened spiritually. Over and over, we will come close to what Jesus wants, but each time we turn back at the true time of testing until we are determined to abandon ourselves to God in total surrender. If we are ever going to do anything worthwhile, there will be times when we must risk everything and leap in the dark.

In the spiritually realm, Jesus Christ demands that we risk everything we hold on to or believe through common sense and leap by faith into what he said. Once we obey, we will find that what he says is consistent as common sense. Trust completely in the Lord, and when he brings you to a new opportunity of adventure, offering it to you, see that you take it.

"Come to Me"

The questions that truly matter in life are remarkably few, and they are answered by these words": "Come to Me" (Matt. 11:28, NKJV). God words are not "Do this" or "Don't do that," but "Come to Me." If we simply come and surrender to Jesus, our life will be brought into harmony with our real desires. But look how difficult it is for us to come to Jesus. We would rather do anything than this one childlike thing, "Come to Me."

Jesus himself is the test of our genuineness. In the most unexpected moments in our lives, there is the whisper of the Lord, "Come to Me," and we are immediately drawn to him. The attitude necessary for us to come to him is one where we have the determination to let go of everything and deliberately commit it all to him. Surrender to him, "and I will give you rest." That is, "I will sustain you, cause you to stand firm. I will get you out of bed, out of your exhaustion, and out of your condition of being half dead while you are still alive." If you give God your rights to yourself, he will make a holy experiment out of you, and his experiment always succeeds.

MAURINE MCFARLANE

Prayer of Surrender

Dear Heavenly Father,

I bring to you my petitions, but I give to you my heart.

While I plead for you to answer my prayers,

I also submit to your will so that my

heart may be strengthened, and your work be done.

Lord, you know just how rebellious I have been.

I ask your forgiveness for manipulating circumstances

and people for trying to manipulate you to get my own way.

May your will be done in my life, even as it is in heaven.

Lord, I want to follow you.

I am putting aside my own desires and conveniences.

I yield my desires that are not in your plan for me.

Even in the midst of my fear, I surrender and entrust my future to you.

This I pray in the name of Jesus.

Amen.

CHAPTER ELEVEN

WHO IS THE HOLY SPIRIT?

In the beginning of creation as written in the book of Genesis 1:26 (NKJV), God said, "Let Us make man in Our image, according to Our likeness; and let them rule over the fish and over the cattle and over all the earth, and over every creeping thing that creeps on the earth. The *us* represents the Trinity, the Father, Son, and the Holy Spirit, which is the blessed third person in the trinity. There are several verses in the Old Testament where God speaks as a plurality.

Regarding Genesis 1:26 (NKJV), those who deny the Trinity say that when God says, "Let Us make," he is speaking with the angels in mind. The problem with this is that angels do not create. There is absolutely no biblical evidence that angels created anything at all. We see in Isaiah 44:24 (NKJV), "Thus says the Lord, your Redeemer, and the One who formed you from the womb, 'I, the Lord, am the maker of all things, stretching out the heavens by Myself, And spreading out the earth all alone.'" God made all things alone. Therefore, the "us" in "Let Us make man in our image" cannot be the angels.

Furthermore, people are not created in the image of angels but of God. *Furthermore*, notice in the fourth verse above, Isaiah 6:8 (NKJV), that God is speaking in the singular and then switches to the plural. He says, "Whom shall I send, and who will go for Us?" This on the unusual construction: the singular speaker refers to himself in the plural.[1]

The personality of the Holy Spirit of God is a person, as much as the Father and Son are persons, and therefore experiences all the sinless elements involved within a divine personality. In the scripture, there are several names and titles given to the Holy Spirit that will provide much insight into his true nature. *He is called the Spirit of God.* Every person has the spirit of God in them. When God formed man of dust from the ground, he breathed into his nostrils the birth of life, and man became a living being (Gen. 2:7, NKJV). We also became an extension of God

"Know ye are the temple of God, and that the Spirit of God dwelleth in you" (1 Cor. 3:16, NKJV). No wonder God requires us to worship him in spirit and in truth. "God is spirit, and those who worship him must worship in spirit and truth" (John 4:24, NKJV). It does not say we can worship God any way we want, *but we "must worship Him in spirit and in truth."* The word "must" makes it absolute. There is no other way we can worship God and be acceptable to him. The word "must," according to *Webster's Dictionary*, expresses "an obligation, a requirement, a necessity, a certainty, and something that must be done." When "must" is used, it means that it is not optional. Here the word "must" expresses that in spirit and in truth is the only way to acceptably worship God.

God seeks true worshippers, and he identifies them as those who "worship Him in spirit and in truth." Worshipping God in spirit and in truth is a serious matter, which must not be taken lightly.[1]

Through the centuries, many of Christ's followers have been ordinary people. Nothing spectacular ever happened to them or through them. Then as it happened to Peter on the day of Pentecost, when he was filled with the Holy Spirit, their lives were dramatically changed. No longer ordinary or average, they became men and women of God, bold in faith and instruments of God's power. Today the same Holy Spirit with his life-changing power is available to each of us. Yet tragically multitudes of Christians go through life without ever experiencing the abundant and fruitful life that Christ promised to all who trust him.

There are times when we sometimes feel that no one understands us or cares about our problems. But God does! He knows just what we need. He loves us so much that he sent his Holy Spirit to be our special friend and helper. With the Holy Spirit as our friend, we will never need to feel lonesome or helpless again. Jesus promised to send another helper. The word he used in Greek was *Paraclete*, which is sometimes translated to comforter. It means, "Someone called alongside to help." The other titles of the Paraclete show you what his powers and responsibilities are and how he will help us. He is called the Spirit of life, the Holy Spirit or Holy Ghost, the Spirit of truth, the Spirit of wisdom, the Spirit of Christ, and the Spirit of God. Whatever our problem may be, our helper has the solution.[2]

The Holy Spirit is also called *the Eternal Spirit*. Hebrews 9:14 (NKJV) says, "How much more through the blood of Christ who through the eternal spirit offered Himself without spot to God, purge your conscience from death works to serve the living God." The solemn transactions between God and man are sometimes called a covenant, here a testament, which is a willing deed of a person, bestowing legacies on such persons as are described, and it only takes effect upon his death. Thus, Christ died not only to obtain the blessings of salvation for us but also to give power to the disposal of them.

All, by sin, became guilty before God and had forfeited everything that is good. But God, willing to show the greatness of his mercy, proclaimed a covenant of grace. Nothing could be cleaned to a sinner, not even his religious duties, except as his guilt was done away by the death of a sacrifice, of value sufficient for that end, and unless he continually depended upon it. For where a covenant is, there must be the death of the one who made it.[2]

He is the Spirit of truth. The promise Jesus makes in John 16: 5–7 (KJV) is "But now I go my way to him that sent me; and none of you asketh me, Whither goest thou? But because I have said these things unto you, sorrow hath filled your heart. Nevertheless, I tell you the truth; it is expedient for you that I go away: for if I go not away, the Comforter will not come unto you; but if I depart, I will send him unto you."

Christ's departure was necessary to the comforter's coming. Sending the Spirit was to be the fruit of Christ's death, which was his going away. His bodily presence could only be in one place at one time, but his Spirit is everywhere, in all places, at all times, wherever two or three are gathered in his name. See here the office of the Spirit, first to reprove or to convince. Convincing work is the Spirit's work; he can do it effectually, and none but him. It is the method the Holy Spirit takes, first to convince and then to comfort.

The Spirit shall convince the world of sin, not merely tell them of it. The Holy Spirit proves that the entire world is guilty before God. He convinces the world of righteousness, that Jesus of Nazareth was Christ the righteous. Also of Christ's righteousness, imparted to us for justification and salvation. Christ's ascension proves the ransom was accepted, and the righteousness finished, through which believers were to be justified of judgment because the prince of this world is judged. All will be well when his power is broken, who made all the mischief. As Christ subdues Satan, this gives us confidence, for no other power can stand before him.[3]

He is the Spirit of grace. The work of the Spirit of God relates directly to the grace of God. It is impossible to walk in the grace of God without the work of the Spirit of God. Whenever the Spirit of God is at work in us, it is the grace of God that is being provided. The word of the Lord to his people was "Not by might, nor by power, but by My Spirit." The Holy Spirit must be the dynamic agent in the work of building Christ's church.

This scripture references a time when Zerubbabel was leading the people back from captivity into the Promised Land so that they would rebuild the temple of God. This act was to be done not by the might and power of man but by the work of the Holy Spirit. Today we are the temple of the Living God. The building up of the church, the building up of our lives is not by our might or power but by the work of the very Spirit of God.[3]

If you allow him, the Holy Spirit can be an active participant of your everyday life. He will reveal things to you before they happen. He will warn you about the unexpected and stop danger before it befalls you. When my daughter Crystal was in high school, she was not allowed to date until she reached twelfth grade and turned seventeen years old. I walked into the house one evening, and Crystal was on the phone talking. I was about to approach her to say hello when the Holy Spirit said to me, "Crystal is dating." At that time in my walk, I did not know how to respond favorably to the things the Lord revealed to me, especially when it came to my children. So I overreacted a little. "Crystal! Are you dating?" "Yes," she said. "When were you going to tell me?" I replied. "It's been only two days," she said. "Oh ok, we can talk about it later," I said. My children could not get away with a thing, especially my son. The Holy Spirit would tell me their business.

The Holy Spirit does the same with me as well. When I was writing my first book, he would choose the books I read, the articles I referenced in the book, and what research materials I would use. He would let me know when I needed to change or improve on a chapter. Each Sunday morning, as part of an assignment the Lord gave me over six years ago, I make Sunday dinner and have an open house where anyone can come to eat. When it first started, I just served families and friends. On any given Sunday, I did not know who would show up. I woke up at 4:00 a.m. to start cooking, and after so many Sundays, I ran out of ideas about what to make or how to make the same things differently.

It still amazes me how the Holy Spirit would give me these wonderful cooking tips and suggestions, and they always turn out great. It is like having a friend with me in the early mornings in the kitchen. I would laugh with him, talk with him, and sometimes I would give him a compliment, telling him what a good job he did. At other times, he would just be silent.

I could write a book on my experiences with the Holy Spirit, but for now I will share this story. Several years ago, I did not work too far from home, so I decided, as part of my exercise, I would walk halfway to work and take the bus the other half. It was five thirty on a winter morning; I was walking on Germantown Avenue, just across from New Covenant Church of Philadelphia. My sneaker lace became undone. I bent down to tie it back up, then the Holy Spirit said to me, "He is coming across the street." I stood up and turned to look on the other side of the street to see who he was talking about.

On the other side of the street was a tall man, and he proceeded to come toward me. My first instinct was to run, but then I thought if I ran, he could block me. What do I do? And he kept coming toward me. Halfway across the street, I started to plea the blood of Jesus. He was now inches away from me. He made a sudden turn away from me and kept going. I never knew I could walk so fast. When I felt safe, I turned back to see where he was. He also turned to look back at the same time, and the look he gave me told me he was scared. I thought, "What did he see when he looked at me?" Whatever it was scared the heck out of him.

I learned later that there was a man early in the mornings on Germantown Avenue who was sexually assaulting woman and young girls on their way to school or work. However, after that morning, I never heard about any such incident anymore. I guess the Lord took care of him. What am I saying here? The Lord said he would send us a comforter and a helper, and if we allow him, he will be whatever we need him to be.

On our own, we struggle even to cry out to God for help. So like the disciples of Jesus, we must ask. Thankfully, God has given us his Holy Spirit as a helper who "will teach us all things" (John 14:26, NKJV). And when we do not know how we should pray, "the Spirit Himself makes intercession for us with groanings which cannot be uttered." Thanks to the help of the Holy Spirit and our savior's sacrifice, we can come boldly in prayer before the throne of grace (Heb. 4:16, NKJV).

The Apostle Paul summarized it well: "For through Christ we all have access by one Spirit to the Father" (Eph. 2:18, NKJV). May we continually pray in the Spirit, as scripture commands. So why are so many Christians not filled with the Holy Spirit? Basically the reason most is that they are unwilling to surrender their wills to God. When God gives his word to us, it includes his thoughts. We can hear God's voice, read God's Word, and because of the thought patterns in our carnal minds, we do not arrive at the meaning of what God is saying. If we do not have the input of the "things of the Spirit" and understand how the Holy Spirit teaches, "comparing Spiritual with spiritual," we are left with interpretation accomplished only by the wisdom of men. Yes, the Bible says that we are to study and rightly divide the Word of God.[4]

1. *According to each of the following verses, give one reason so few Christians are filled— directed and empowered—with the Holy Spirit. (Psalm 119:105, Proverbs 16:18; Proverbs 29:25; Luke 9:26)*

2. *What is another barrier between you and the Lord that keeps you from being filled with the Spirit? (Psalm 66:18) What else can divert you from being filled with the Spirit? (1 John 2:15–17)*

3. *Lack of trust in God will also keep you from being filled with the Holy Spirit. Read John 3:16, Romans 8:32 and 1 John 3:16. Describe how these verses help you trust God fully.[4]*

Open Prayer

Dear Father, I need you.

I acknowledge that I have been directing my own

life and that, as a result, I have sinned against you.

I thank you that you have forgiven my sins through Christ's

death on the cross for me.

I now invite you to again take your place on the throne of my life.

Fill me with the Holy Spirit as you commanded me to be filled.

I pray this in the name of Jesus.

As an expression of my faith, I thank you for taking control of

my life and for filling me with the Holy Spirit.

Father, I thank you for your great and abounding grace.

Thank you that your Holy Spirit is there to explain and to

deliver the grace of God.

And, Lord, for any among us who do not know the

Lord Jesus Christ as Lord and Savior and have not had

new birth by the Spirit of God, stir their hearts even right

now to say "Lord Jesus, forgive me, a sinner."

By your Spirit, send us new life. For all of us who might

in any measure need a new filling, Lord, we humbly ask

you to fill us again. Fill us so that we would overflow.

We bring to you, Lord Jesus, our thirsts, needs, and yearnings.

We believe that you can meet them.

Quench our thirst by your Holy Spirit and continue to

do this work as we believe in you so that you would fill

us with living water that it might flow out to others

who need a touch from you. Lord, let us not desire to

resist, quench, or grieve your Spirit.

We pray that you would work by your Spirit in our lives.

In Jesus's name, I pray,

Amen.

ENDNOTES:

1   Christian Apologetics, "Let Us Make Man in Our Image."

2   Matthew Henry, *Matthew Henry's Concise Commentary on the Whole Bible*, Hebrews 9:15–22.

3   Bob Hoekstra, "The Holy Spirit and the Grace of God," *Blue Letter Bible*, accessed July 11, 2013, https://www.blueletterbible. org/Comm/hoekstrabob/grace/grace04.cfm.

4   Bill Bright, "Why So Few Christians Are Filled with the Holy Spirit," *Cru*, https://www.cru.org/us/en/train-and-grow/10-basic-steps/3-the-holy-spirit.3.html.

CHAPTER TWELVE

HOW WORSHIPPING GOD INCREASES OUR FAITH

Many of us on our faith journey will not know or will be confused by the difference between praising God and worshipping God. I believe it is imperative to take the time to explain the difference to help you bring a new depth in the way you honor God. Praise does not require anything of us; it is merely the truthful acknowledgment of the righteous acts of another. We can praise our family, friends, boss, and children, but praising God is the joyful recounting of all God has done for us. It is closely intertwined with thanksgiving as we offer back to God appreciation for his mighty works on our behalf.

According to Psalm 89:5 (NKJV), all inhabitants of the earth are instructed to praise the Lord. In scripture, praise is usually presented as boisterous, joyful, and uninhibited. God invites praise of all kinds from his creation. Jesus said that if people do not praise God, even the "stones will cry out" (Luke 19:40, NKJV). We can praise him with singing (Isa. 12:5; Ps. 9:11, NKJV), with shouting (Ps. 33:1, 98:4, NKJV), with dancing (Ps. 150:4, NKJV), and with using musical instruments (1 Chron. 13:8; Ps. 108:2, 150:3–5, NKJV).[1]

Worship, however, comes from a different place within our spirit. Worship should be reserved for God alone (Luke 4:8, NKJV). Worship is the art of losing self in the adoration of another. Praise can be a part of worship, but worship goes beyond praise. Praise is easy; worship is not. Worship gets to the heart of who we are. To truly worship God, we must let go of our self-worship. We must be willing to humble ourselves before God, surrender every part of our lives to his control, and adore him for who he is, not just what he has done. Worship is a lifestyle, not just an occasional activity.[2]

Jesus said the Father is seeking those who will worship him "in spirit and in truth" (John 4:23, NKJV). Worshipping God is not about a ritual or prayer repetition. It is not about spending a few minutes a day reading our Bible or about reciting our wish list daily. True worship requires total commitment of our body, mind, and spirit. It is about exalting, adoring, and acknowledging the God of the Bible. It has nothing to do with religion, but it has everything to do with having an intimate and profound relationship with God the Father, Son, and Holy Spirit.

I believe the most important way to show our devotion to God is through our everyday lives. When we strive to be Christlike, loving and serving others, to honoring and glorifying God, then we are truly worshipping him. The secret of worship is in doing everything "as unto the Lord." The Bible says, "Because of God's great mercy to us I appeal to you: Offer yourselves as…dedicated to His service and pleasing to Him" (Rom. 12:1, GNT). That is what it means to worship! When we fail to worship God, we always find a substitute, even if it ends up being ourselves.

Worship is a universal urge, hardwired by God into every fiber of our being. It is as natural as breathing. There are times in church when I hear someone say, "I did not get anything out of it." A person like that worshipped for the wrong reason! Yes, there are personal benefits, but we do not worship to please ourselves. Our highest motive should be to exalt God in whatever we do.

Where Do We Worship?

The example of how Jesus answers this very question to the Samaritan woman at the well responds to our question today. During his conversation with this woman beside the well, she brought up a very touchy subject between the Samaritans and the Jews: Where is the correct place to worship God? She said, "Our fathers worshiped on this mountain, and you Jews say that in Jerusalem is the place where one ought to worship" (John 4:20, NKJV). But instead of taking one side or the other, Jesus gave this woman the proper perspective. Jesus said to her, "Woman, believe Me, the hour is coming when you will neither on this mountain, nor in Jerusalem, worship the Father…But the hour is coming, and now is, when the true worshipers will worship the Father in spirit and truth; for the Father is seeking such to worship Him. God is Spirit, and those who worship Him must worship in spirit and truth" (John 4:21, 23–24, NKJV).

Not only did Jesus disregard both sides of this centuries-old debate, but he also revealed that this woman's whole perception of worship was severely skewed. She was concerned with the traditional, religious activities of "worship." But God is not pleased by works that outwardly appear righteous unless they result from a heart that is inwardly submitted to him. Interestingly the Greek word translated to "worship" in this passage refers to service at the temple, but Jesus reapplies it. Instead of worship in a physical temple at a particular place, we ought to worship God "in spirit and in truth."

The New Testament reveals that our bodies are the temple of God (1 Cor. 3:16, NKJV), so worship should take place everywhere we go.[3] We can worship God in church, in the garden, while we are shopping, or in the shower. Location does not matter or how many people are involved. Worship can be done with a group of people or by yourself.[3]

When we come before the Lord with a pure and repentant heart, he will bless us with his grace and mercy. We can worship God through praying, singing, raising our hands in adoration, dancing, making arts, using colors, playing instruments, using flags and banners, and even through being in ministry. Jesus promised he would always be with us (Heb. 13:5, NKJV), that his presence would be with us when we gather in his name (Matt. 18:20, NKJV), and here we are, promised that we enter the presence of God, in a very special way, when we are worshipping and praising him. You can sense the presence of God in a powerful way as you are worshipping.

I have always been able to tell an expressed difference when I am putting all I have into my worship experience as opposed to when I am not. We enter heaven (the presence of God) through praise and worship.

When Moses left God's presence, his face was glowing (Exod. 34, NKJV). As Solomon worshipped the Lord, the cloud of the glory of God so filled the temple that the priest could no longer stand to minister (1 Kings 8:11; 2 Chron. 5:6, 7:1–4, NKJV). What might it be like when we worship him with all our might? How will we be affected by his presence? Every experience in God's presence may be somewhat different. One thing I am assured of is that in his "presence is fullness of joy; At Your right hand are pleasures forevermore" (Ps. 16:11, NKJV).[3]

As I worshipped the Lord at a camp meeting in Arlington, Virginia, I was taken up to another dimension, where Jesus danced with me, and then he led me through a door, where there were the most beautiful flowers I have ever seen. When we worship the Lord with all our being, we never know where the spirit will take us.

During Seasons of Darkness

As a follower of Jesus Christ, I can personally tell you that these seasons of darkness are not only common, but they are also necessary for our maturity. This is the time I describe as not "feeling" God. This experience can be quite disheartening and discouraging for believers, especially for those like myself whose conversion was a sensational experience. I would have spiritual highs and spiritual lows. My faith would be shaken if I had a day where I could not "feel" God. The way I would gauge a worship set or a sermon would be based upon how it made me feel and whether I could feel God. I have heard people say that, "The Holy Spirit really showed up when we started singing, 'Shout to the Lord!'"—a prime example of how we perceive God's presence through feelings.

As I have wrestled through these seasons and encouraged others going through them, I found there is much to be gleamed from these perceived silences from God. If we could always feel God, why would we need to have faith? After all, the scripture from Hebrews 11:1 (NKJV) says that we need increased hope and conviction for our faith to increase. Here is how I learned to come through my season of darkness:

- If you have reached this far in this book, then you are beginning to learn something about God, just a little something because we can truly never know God beyond what he has revealed to us. Remember, God is not just something to feel, but he is also someone to know. Our need to feel God is often a sign that we need to know him more.

- Confess and repent. There are times that our sin hinders our fellowship with God. If we are sensitive to notice a distancing of his presence, let us make sure it isn't us who have caused this separation.
- Fortunately, God's grace abounds, and our salvation is secure. With this confidence, we can confess our sins and trust in his gracious forgiveness (1 John 1:9, NKJV).
- Jesus must be the prize. We are all guilty of longing for the benefits of God at the expense of the presence and person of God. It is important to rejoice that the reality and existence of God are not contingent on how we are feeling. Instead God's grace can be illustrated further in his desire that we mature in our faith and not stay in the same place.
- Continue the pursuit through worship. If our goal is to know God more than just to feel God, then we must continue to get to know him through prayer, worship, community, and intentional time in his word. This is where your faith is tested and ultimately strengthened. Continuing to pursue and obey despite not feeling God is like adding more weight to the bar as you exercise. It will be difficult, it may hurt, but it is worth it in the long run.

Rejoice as this lack of feeling becomes even more pronounced in moments when we are going through trials. See James 1:2–4 (NKJV). James tells his readers to rejoice in their trials because it is in these times that our faith increases or becomes complete. Those times of not feeling God are helpful in the long run and are meant for God's glory and for our good. This is not to say that this it is easy, but if we desire to mature in our faith, we must expect our faith to be tested and tried.[3]

The good news is this: the season does not last forever, and it will ultimately amount to increased faith and greater intimacy with God.

Psalm 145

A psalm of praise of David.

I will exalt you, my God the King;

I will praise your name for ever and ever.

Every day I will praise you

and extol your name for ever and ever.

Great is the LORD and most worthy of praise; his greatness no one can fathom.

One generation commends your works to another; they tell of your mighty acts.

They speak of the glorious splendor of your majesty

and I will meditate on your wonderful works.

They tell of the power of your awesome works and I will proclaim your great deeds.

They celebrate your abundant goodness and joyfully sing of your righteousness.

The LORD is gracious and compassionate, slow to anger and rich in love.

The LORD is good to all; he has compassion on all he has made.

All your works praise you, LORD.

your faithful people extol you.

They tell of the glory of your kingdom and speak of your might,

so that all people may know of your mighty acts and the glorious splendor of your kingdom.

Your kingdom is an everlasting kingdom,

and your dominion endures through all generations.

The LORD is trustworthy in all he promises and faithful in all he does.

The LORD upholds all who fall and lifts up all who are bowed down.

The eyes of all look to you,

and you give them their food at the proper time.

You open your hand

and satisfy the desires of every living thing.

The LORD is righteous in all his ways

and faithful in all he does.

The LORD is near to all who call on him, to all who call on him in truth.

He fulfills the desires of those who fear him; he hears their cry and saves them.

The LORD watches over all who love him, but all the wicked he will destroy.

My mouth will speak in praise of the LORD.

Let every creature praise his holy name for ever and ever.

ENDNOTES

1   http://www.gotquestions.org/difference-praise-worship. html#ixzz2bxidmpyD.

2   http://www.gotquestions.org/difference-praise-worship.html#ixzz2bxidmpyD.

3   Gary Linton, "The Purpose of Praise and Worship," *Ministrymaker* magazine.

CHAPTER THIRTEEN

THE SUPERNATURAL

We live in a world today that is fascinated by the unknown; the things we cannot see but believe exist. Millions of dollars are spent in Hollywood making movies and television shows that try to depict and understand the supernatural world. I cannot say I blame them; the idea of knowing something before it shows up in the natural or physical world is great power for a person. It means if you can see it, then you can do something about it; you could change the outcome. Now that is power! Hollywood is not real; it is fiction, so the movies and TV shows are just someone's idea of what they think or imagine the supernatural world is about, and it is usually dark. *In case you are wondering, what does the supernatural has to do with "How to pray to get what I need?"* Everything! Because everything in the universe is created twice. Before you see it in the natural, it was first created in the supernatural.

So what is the supernatural? Let's first examine the different definitions, according to *Wikipedia*. The *supernatural* (Medieval Latin: *supernātūrālis*: *supra* "above," naturalis "nature," first used in AD 1520–30) is that which is not subject to the laws of physics or, more figuratively, that which is said to exist above and beyond nature. In philosophy, popular culture, and fiction, the supernatural is associated with the paranormal, religions, and occultism.[1,2]

In our life here on earth, there are experiences, trials, and manifestations that cannot be explained to natural causes. These trials and experiences must be explained by referring to something beyond the natural realm, beyond that which we know from our five senses; this is the supernatural. The term "naturalism" refers to the system of thought, which holds that all phenomena can be explained in terms of natural causes and laws, without attributing supernatural significance to them. For the person who holds to naturalism, talk about "God in heaven" does not make sense, since God cannot be weighed or measured and is not subject to the scientific method. To the naturalist, "God" is merely the product of the imagination, the projection of human wishes and hope. The person such as I who holds to supernaturalism, by way of contrast, believes that God is above humans and is free to act upon (and within) nature however he pleases.[1]

I understand why most people are committed to the idea that all things can be explained that the ultimate judge of truth is the human mind, and that if the human mind cannot make sense of any matter, it simply cannot exist. But people of faith like myself who believe that the supernatural power of God begins with creation realize there is not a single law in science that will account for the creation of anything. We must go back to Genesis— "In the beginning God created." He speaks it, and it came into existence; that is supernatural creation.

Science has been trying to deny that God created the world supernaturally by speaking it. "The man of science thus starts with two things. If we ask him this question, *'What do you say was the beginning?'* he will answer, 'Matter and motion.' But we must go back further and ask, *"Who created matter, and who started motion?"* Even if we accept the Nebular Hypothesis of Pierre Simon de Laplace, we are compelled to start with existing matter and existing motion. 'Every effect must have its adequate cause.' This is the teaching of Genesis 1:1 NKJV."

"The word 'supernatural' is not used in the Bible, but it has an important function in defining some of scripture. For example, when God speaks to humans, when Jesus descended to the human level in the Incarnation, and when Jesus was raised from the dead, these properly are designated as supernatural events. They are totally unexplainable by regular sources of human understanding."[3]

There are hundreds of examples in scripture that tell of God's power in action. These accounts interaction between the visible world that we can see and touch and the invisible world that scripture tells us is there and is real, such as his mighty acts parting of the Red Sea (Exod. 14:21–23, NKJV), the giving of the Ten Commandments on Mt. Sinai (Exod. 19:16–18, NKJV), and the ten plagues of Egypt. These are fabulous examples of God's power that shape and fashion history. This type of divine power is true all the way through the scriptures, and it is true in our lives as well. What is amazing is that if we believe in him, he promises to instill a small portion of that same immense power in our hearts (Deut. 8:18, NKJV). And through that power, he gives us the ability to execute the impossible.

Christianity is simply the manifestation of divine power in the presence of human weakness. Remember Abraham and Sarah? God promised them a son (Gen. 17:16–19, NKJV). According to the laws of nature, it was completely impossible for them to conceive. Yet the Lord said to them, "Is anything too hard for Me? At the time appointed I will return unto thee and Sarah shall have a son" (Gen. 18:14, KJV). Something totally impossible was about to be made possible by the power of God (Luke 1:37, NKJV). And of course Sara ended up conceiving and bringing forth a son, who would play a major role in God's plan for mankind.

What is the source behind the supernatural power? Hebrews 1:3 (NKJV) tells us that God upholds *all* things by the word of his power. Think about what this is really saying. God sustains everything in the universe by his hand of power. In other words, *all* he has to do is speak his will, and his power will then accomplish it (Ps. 33:9, NKJV). For example, he formed the mountains by his power. He divided the seas by his power. He divided the light from the darkness by his power (Gen. 1:4, NKJV). He created man by his power (Gen. 1:26, NKJV). And he will quicken the dead and call them to life by his power (Rom. 4:17, NKJV).

The source of all power therefore is God. It is *his* saving power, *his* pardoning power (Matt. 9:6, NKJV), *his* infinite power (Matt. 28:18, NKJV), his power over nature (Luke 8:24, NKJV), and his lifegiving power (John 17:2; John 10:10, NKJV). Romans 13:1 (NKJV) tells us, "For there is no power but of God." He is the one who places rulers in positions of power, and he is the one who controls our lives and our destinies by his power.[3]

How does God's supernatural power manifest itself in our lives today? The way God's divine power was manifested in the Old Testament was by miraculous deeds, where a special and sometimes temporary anointing often accompanied these miracles, as with Moses, Samson, Elijah, Elisha, and so on. Today we read about the incredible outpouring of the Spirit and the miracles that are happening in China, Africa, and other countries. There are many Christians who do not believe in the supernatural. I do not understand considering that Jesus embodies the supernatural. It is like creating Jesus in their own image, which does not really work. It is spiritually empty, and it is an attempt to have something that never was and never can be. It is Christianity without Christ. It would be comforting to the modern mind to have Jesus without angels, demons, and exorcisms.

The problem is twofold. First, it is simply historically inaccurate, or more specifically, it is untrue. The Jesus of the Gospels is a miracle worker. He heals the sick, raises the dead, exorcises demons, and was tempted by Satan. *Just how prevalent is the supernatural in the Gospels?* It is evident that the Gospel of Matthew is filled with supernatural acts, beings, and occurrences. Matthew is not alone in this version of events. The synoptic Gospels (Matthew, Mark, and Luke) record many of the exact same events.

In my opinion, you cannot believe in the bodily resurrection of Jesus, including the empty tomb, and deny the supernatural. Similarly you cannot deny the resurrection and believe in the supernatural if you are a Christian. The Gospel of John does not record as many miracles, but its presentation of Jesus is more supernatural. For example, is the opening two paragraphs in the Gospel of John:

In the beginning was the Word, and the Word was with God,
and the Word was God. He was in the beginning with God.
All things were made through Him, and without Him nothing was made that was made.
In Him was life, and the life was the light of men.
And the light shines in the darkness,
and the darkness did not comprehend it (John 1:1–5, NKJV).

John is referring to Jesus as the "Word." He makes the claim that Jesus existed in the beginning with God prior to the creation of the world. He further claims that everything that was made was made through Jesus. Finally, he claims that Jesus contains life within him, and this life is the light of men. In the first two paragraphs of the Gospel of John, we see Jesus presented as the supernatural, eternal, creator of the universe, and the light of mankind.[3]

When the Natural Meets the Supernatural

What do I mean by "supernatural?" Here is what I mean by it: the realm of activity of unseen agents unknowable by science because it is "above" nature. By "above," I do not mean literally, spatially above; I mean transcends, goes beyond. Add to that supernatural events, "miracles," ones that are in principle unable to be explained by science or predicted by the scientist, even one who has all the information possible about the context and applicable natural laws. Believers who are filled with the Holy Spirit and believe in the resurrection power of Jesus Christ will have experiences in the supernatural, where they will literally transcend to the beyond. The person who denies it—that is, denies miracles—is seriously distorting, truncating, if not rejecting, authentic Christianity.[3]

Paul in 2 Corinthians 12:2 (NKJV) talks about his third heaven experience. I, too, had such an experience; in fact, I had two such experiences. Prior to the last two years I have kept a recorded journal, I wanted to record my spiritual journey, especially those considered beyond this world. The encounters described below are documented and are true.

My supernatural experiences began immediately after I committed my life to Jesus Christ. I was enthralled by God; I wanted to know everything about him. I would watch every person on the television who would preach the word or talk or teach about him. I could not get enough of this Jesus. I would read the Bible daily for hours. I just wanted to know and be one with him. I was desperate for the presence of God; I want to see him and experience him the way Moses did.

In fact, this is funny; consider the change in my attitude after that moment. The first statement I made to the Lord after what Christianity call "born again" is that "I did not want to read the Bible." I did not want to know about him from the preacher. I wanted him to show up in my house in the living room right there and then, just as he did for Moses. Of course he did not show up, at least not the way I requested. I did not see him, but I waited because I believed if he could show up as a burning bush for Moses, he can show up in my living room to me. I learned shortly after that God shows up in our lives when he chooses to do it and how he chooses to do so, but he will show up. That is the moment the journey of my life began.

Before this experience, I have had several supernatural experiences and had received many visions in my life but none that took me to the third heaven, so I will focus on this experience. I was in worship with the Lord as I always do each morning, and as I read the second book of Kings about the false prophets and what God would do to them for lying to the people of God, I became concerned about things I have told people of what God said. I never declared to be a prophet, but God do speak to me, and at times, he would give me instructions for someone.

Because I was new to the experience of hearing from God, I began to wonder if I heard from God, or if I was listening to the "devil," which basically means my own thoughts.

I went into the powder room and looked at my reflection in the mirror, saying out loud to myself, "What will this do to my faith if I am wrong about what I told these people, and more importantly, what will it do to their faith?" My concern was so strong that suddenly I had the urge to go to the altar in my living room and pray. The altar is the place in my living room, namely, the sofa, where I pray and worship each morning.

Shortly after I began to pray, I heard a suction sound as if I were suctioned up, and before I knew it, I was in another place. I was not sure where I was, but I noticed many crowns floating above me in a straight line, the type of crowns kings wore in the Old Testaments. I thought, "It is true. We do wear crowns in heaven."

Then something happened. The heavens began to open, and the most amazing palace emerges out of the heaven, of great beauty of multicolor stones of emeralds, diamond, and rubies, and some of which I do not know the names. I began to point my finger, asking the question, *"Do you see it?"* I repeat it several times to apparently someone who was standing next to me, even though I never turned to look at him. He did not answer me, but I continued to ask, *"Do you see it?"*

Next I knew, I was taken up into the palace, standing before the entrance of a room. It reminded me of the entrance of a room from the biblical days where the arch is curved. No door was attached to the entrance as if I could just enter in freely. I stood at the entrance, looking inside. It was very bright and not the type of light we know on earth, much different. And in the room were many sheep, and I heard myself speaking to the person who stood next to me. I still never looked at him, but through my peripheral vision, I saw that he is wearing a long white gown. Then I said to him, *"Do you believe me now?"* Once again, he did not answer me. I stepped into the room where the sheep and bright lights were, then I realized I had to leave, but I did not want to. Before I could object, I was back in my living room.

Strangely, when I returned, I was afraid. With my eyes closed, I took the blanket from the sofa and covered my head. I did not want to see; I was afraid of what I would see when I removed the blanket. After a little while, I gently removed the blanket and saw that I was back in the living room of my home. "Oh god, I must tell somebody about this," I thought, marching back and forth in the living room. I repeated, "God, I have to tell someone. *Who can I call?*" Then I heard the voice of the Lord said, "Call Sharon and Hilary."

Sharon is someone I met years ago who is a strong woman of God with a doctorate in theology. At the time, she was visiting family in the South, so I did not expect her to answer her phone, but she did. I explained to her what I had just experienced. She then explained to me about the third heaven experience of Paul and told me I just had mine. Before that moment, I had never heard of a third heaven experience.

Once I hung up the phone with Sharon, I called Hilary, with whom I had connected with from the moment we met at New Covenant Church of Philadelphia. Hilary is my pastor's sister and a prayer warrior in the Kingdom of God. Hilary's response to my experience was much different from Sharon's, which is why God told me to call each of them. Hilary said, "Let's pray," and she prayed. When she was finished, I felt so much better. The fear I had when I returned was gone, even though it took me two weeks to feel normal again.

After that experience, I felt the molecules in my body wore off, as if when I heard that suction sound before I was taking up, it was me leaving my body, and when I returned, it took a while to adjust. As you can imagine, I thought about this experience repeatedly, wondering what it meant when I asked God that question at the entrance before I went into the room. *"Do you believe me now?"* Why do I need to ask God such a question when he knows everything? Because I did not know before that day what a third heaven experience was, I began to read about Paul's experience in relations to my own experience. More importantly, I wanted to know why God allowed me to experience this important thing and what he wanted me to do with it.

Beyond Paul's experience, is this even biblical? Can we find different levels or dimensions of heaven in the Bible? These are many of the questions I had. The reality is quite simple. The term "heaven" is used in three different ways throughout the Bible. The first refers to the atmosphere around the earth, such as when the "windows of heaven" were opened (see Gen. 1:8, 7:11, NKJV). The second refers to outer space, including the planets and stars. These "heavens" are often referred to in the plural (see Gen. 1:1, NKJV). The third refers to the dwelling place of God (see Rev. 16:11, 19:1, NKJV).

Therefore, when Paul describes being "caught up to the third heaven," he is describing his experience as a prophet, seeing a heavenly vision. The Holy Spirit transported him to heaven itself to learn divine things directly from God, in much the same way that Ezekiel and John the Revelator are recorded as receiving visions. The Bible also sheds light on people being taken up in the body and out of the body. In the Old Testament, both Enoch (Gen. 5:24) and Elijah (2 Kings 2:9–12, NKJV) were taken up in bodily form to heaven, though it was permanent for both and not temporary. Yet even before Elijah was permanently taken up to heaven, he was carried from place to place by the Spirit of the Lord (1 Kings 18:12, NKJV).[3]

My second supernatural third heaven experience was much different from the first. It was also with the second experience that I received and understood the answer to my question to God of *"Do you believe me now?"* It was a Friday evening, and I sat at my porch, waiting for seven o'clock to arrive so I could take part in prayer with several churches that were coming together for the first time to pray for the city of Philadelphia. My church did not participate, and I was so disappointed that they chose not to do so because the act of the churches uniting was part of the prophecy for Philadelphia that the Lord had given me for the book *Release the Prophetic*

Destiny in Philadelphia: A City Under Reconstruction. He had me write about Philadelphia and what the church had to do to take back the city from the enemy (the devil).

While I was waiting, I began to worship with the Lord, expressing to him my desires to be part of the change for Philadelphia. I begged the Lord to use me, and like Isaiah, I told him to send me. At 7:00 p.m., I prayed for Philadelphia, all the problems the city had with murders, violence, fatherlessness, you name it. I was praying for change to come to our city. I don't know how long I was out there praying, but I became very tired, so I went into the living room and lay on the sofa, the place I call my altar, where I would meet the Lord for worship. I am sure I fell asleep before my head hit the cushion on the sofa. The next thing I knew, I was taken up in the spirit to heaven, and I was in the presence of God, sitting at his feet.

I did not see anyone, but what I felt was the strong presence of his Spirit. It was so powerful it fills the atmosphere. In a sense, it was extremely overwhelming, much so I could feel the love in my heart just overflowing out of me to him. I have never experienced such a love before; I could literally feel my heart emptying out to him in adoration. Then I asked him, *"Did you know me before I was born?"* And like my first experience, he did not answer me. Instead he took me back to that entrance where I was before, the place of light, and the sheep were in the room.

I stood and looked for a while at the room, and then I finally got it. The question I asked God was not for him; it was for me. The way God teaches us individually is different; now two people experience God the same way. I had a concern, and my God took the time to take me back where I originally came from to show me the commitment I made to him before he formed me in my mother's womb and send me to the world. Apparently when I was with him before I was born, I told the Lord to send me to get those sheep, which represent people. I must have convinced the Lord I could do it, so when I returned with his sheep, I said to him, "Do you believe me now?"

As to say to him, I told you I could do it. Of course God knows all things, but it was for me to know I could do it. I also realized that my yes to the Lord would include every experience I would have on earth, good or bad, on my way to getting his sheep. For the first time in my life, I no longer felt like a victim because I agreed to endure whatever comes my way for the sake of his people. If we only knew how important we are to God and that each of us has a purpose in this world, we would live our lives differently. Like Paul, I recorded the vision and the revelation I received and resumed with my normal life.

I share these experiences with you not to boast or to appear more special than anyone else but so that you can see the supernatural world is not something you can imagine or make up. It is something you can only experience through the power of God, and if we believe in him, he promises to instill a small portion of that same immense power in our hearts (Deut. 8:18, NKJV). And through that power, he gives us the ability to execute the impossible. To repeat what I stated before, Christianity is simply the manifestation of divine power in the presence of human weakness.

What God wants us to know about heaven is revealed in the Bible; as for the rest, "The secret things belong to the Lord our God," as stated in Deuteronomy 29:29 (NKJV), and he reveals it to whom he chooses.

In case you are wondering if you have what it takes for God to reveal his secret things to you, here is what I believe. The true measure of a person of God does not lie in our claims of visions and experiences with God or the force of our personality, the size of our ministry, our educational degrees, or any other human criteria. A true person of God is marked by how much we have suffered in the war against the kingdom of darkness, how concerned we are for people, how humble we are, and how accurately we handle the supernatural revelation found in God's Word (2 Tim. 2:15, NKJV).

Can we be like Paul, such a man patiently endures the suffering and humiliation of this life, knowing that such "momentary, light affliction is producing an eternal weight of glory far beyond all comparison" (2 Cor. 4:17, NKJV)? I must admit it took me a long time to mentally get to that place in my life where I see my afflictions as something good happening to me that will eventually benefit me. Like many of you, I did not understand why I had to go through it. It was challenging, painful, and downright disheartening.

Prayer for the Supernatural

Heavenly Father, thank you for revealing your

secret things to me on the mountaintop.

God, I want to know you. I want more of you—

more of your presence, more of your fullness, and more of

your glory in my life.

Teach me now to take my mountaintop experiences with you

and bring them down to the valley where the hurt,

the suffering, and the afflicted are

that I may with your power transform them

though their sufferings. In Jesus's name,

Amen.

ENDNOTES

1   "Supernatural," dictionary.com, accessed June 30, 2013.
2   "Jump up," *Online Etymology Dictionary*, etymonline.com, accessed June 30, 2013.
3   W. H. Griffith Thomas, "The Supernatural in the Bible," *Brethren Revival Fellowship* 37, 5 (2002).

CHAPTER FOURTEEN

BELIEVING RIGHT IS THE KEY TO VICTORIOUS LIVING

Lack of knowledge always creates dysfunctional thinking, which leads to dysfunctional behavior. If you are struggling today in your life, it is because of what you believe of yourself, and what you believe of yourself has everything to do with what you believe of God. If you really want to know how you think of God, look at the people around you and observe how you treat them and think of them. It is the same way you treat God, just as you do a man, with unbelief and oftentimes contempt.

There is a difference knowing something on a cognitive level than to experiencing it because it is difficult for us to understand the potter's will. Our suffering is caused by what we believe. We are all looking for something greater than ourselves, and the further we are removed from that experience, the greater our longing for truth, love, and God.

When we cannot find our way to the experience we long for, then fear takes its place. Fear dispenses anger, and anger is a lucid way to respond to problem that always leads to the wrong action. In John 10:10 (NKJV), God said, "The thief cometh not but to steal and to kill and to destroy. I am come that they might have life, and that they might have it more abundantly." That is a statement that should rejoice the heart of a child of God, just knowing that he came not just to give us life but also to give it to us more abundantly.

We have a better covenant, established upon better promises, yet we do not possess them automatically. To walk in the abundant life means we must follow certain principles and laws laid out by God to when we are not in obedience we walk in the curse. To be cursed simply means we are not going into the right path; we are not in alignment with the Word of God. *So why do we choose to believe the lies?* The moment we believe a "lie" is the moment the "lie" becomes true in our lives; it's the "truth" that sets you free, the "real" truth (Jesus). He said, "I am the way, the truth, and the life." If we believe anything other than "Jesus," we believe a lie, and the lie we believe becomes our truth, and we are deceived. We begin to exist in deception.

Right believing is all about renewing our mind and uprooting the wrong beliefs that shape our thinking and behavior. God wants to change the way we think by shifting our thoughts from self-occupation to Christ-occupation. If we want to live right, we must believe right. We must see ourselves as our Heavenly Father sees us, as dearly loved and precious. When we allow God's love to saturate our minds, it does not matter what wrong beliefs, fears, or addictions are keeping us bound. His grace will begin to break them down.

Fear is the single biggest problem that most of us face. It pretty much underpins every other problem we face in our life. It is dangerous. It creeps upon us without us even realizing, slowly taking over our lives, until eventually it steals it. It steals our confidence, makes us feel insecure, affects our relationships, and stops us from doing things. It becomes so deeply embedded within us that most of the time, we do not even realize that it is there; it becomes part of who we are.

I try to reflect on my life to find out when the spirit of fear became such a prominent part of it. I realized it was always there, hidden away in the depths of my soul. I did so many stupid things out of fear. With each disappointment, each setback, and each betrayal, it emerges itself more and more in my life.

As Joseph Prince, senior pastor of New Creation Church based in Singapore, explained, "Long before the enemy can steal our victory, he steals our song. Long before he can steal our joy, he steals our praise." Before I knew it, I became critical, pessimistic, moody, and oppressed. I no longer believed what God said about me. Until God began to show me how every incident had a root of fear, it ruled my life. It was fear that pushed me to work so hard, fear that if I stopped, I would not make it. It was fear that made me work hard to be a good mother; the thought of having children who would not be successful and productive in this world was frightful for me. It was fear that motivated me to keep moving. It was also fear of not having enough money that led me to a gambling addiction years ago. These were all the things lacking in my life growing up. There was no foundation to build my life on other than the lies I believed for so long.

In the previous chapter, I mentioned how afraid I was when I returned into my body from my third heaven experience. I hid my head under the blanket for a while until I forced myself to look up. But that was not my first time in the presence of the Lord that I was afraid. One summer night I was walking Pete, our family dog. On the way back to the house, I had to come down the steps that led to a path to the back of the house, where there were many large trees. Suddenly I was stopped in my tracks because the glory was so strong. I knew I was in the presence of God, then I heard myself saying, "God, you are here."

Suddenly, after I acknowledged his presence, I became afraid, ran into the house, and told the reverend Bell, my neighbor who was visiting with us. He directed me to read Isaiah 60. He did not specify a verse, so I read the entire chapter, but for this purpose, I will quote verse 60:1: "Arise, shine; for thy light is come, and the glory of the Lord is risen upon thee."

Why did the enemy use fear as the weapon against us, and why is he successful? Fear, which is doubt, contradicts the Word of God, so if I am afraid, then I don't believe God, and if I don't believe God, there is nothing he can do for me. We can only please God if we have faith, and doubt will always challenge our faith. Fear paralyzes us, sometimes it freezes us, sometimes it causes us to panic, and at times, it makes us invent extraordinary ways to control the events of life or actions of other people. Occasionally we do anything to avoid certain people or episodes.

One of the worst things about fear is that it is contagious. We infect one another. It took God few years to teach me to stop worrying and to trust him. If we serve two masters, ourselves and God, there will be difficulties, combined with doubts and confusion. Our attitude must be one of complete reliance on God. We encounter difficulties when we try to usurp the authority of the Holy Spirit for our own purposes. There are three weapons that we can expect from the devil. The Bible tells us that we struggle not against flesh and blood but against demonic forces. Ephesians 6:12 (NKJV) says, "For we wrestle not against flesh and blood, but against principalities, against powers, against the rulers of the darkness of this world, against spiritual wickedness in high places." The three primary things we struggle against include deceptions, temptations, and accusations.

Deceptions

When the enemy sends deception our way, it is an attempt to deceive us into believing something that is not true, so we will fall into error. Strongholds are built through deception. A stronghold is formed when deception takes hold in a person's mind. A stronghold is an incorrect thinking pattern that stems from believing something that is not true.

Temptations

Temptation often follows deception. First the enemy tells us, "You won't surely die!" then he makes the fruit on the forbidden tree look good to us. Since Eve accepted Satan's deception (his lie), now the tree that she was not supposed to touch looked good to her. She was tempted (enticed) to sin because she allowed herself to first be deceived. Temptation is when we are enticed or encouraged to sin in one way or another.

Accusations

The devil is known as the accuser of the brethren (Rev. 12:10, NKJV). He is known to take a believer who has done an embarrassing or gross sin in their past and continue to rub it in their face and beat them down with guilt and condemnation over their past, even though Jeremiah 31:33–34 (NKJV) states it plain to us: "For this is the covenant that I will make with the house of Israel after those days, declares the LORD: "I will put my law within them, and I will write it on their hearts. And I will be their God, and they shall be my people." And no longer shall each one teach his neighbor and each his brother, saying, 'Know the LORD,' for they shall all know me, from the least of them to the greatest, declares the LORD. For I will forgive their iniquity, and I will remember their sins no more."

Dealing with Deception

We have two weapons to deal with deceptions: the belt of truth (Eph. 6:14, NKJV) and the sword of the Spirit (Eph. 6:17, NKJV), which is the Word of God. Both are truth, which is found in God's Word, so why are they given two different names (a sword and a belt)? Because one is meant to be defensive (the belt), while the other is meant to be offensive (the sword). This means that the Word of God is both an offensive and a defensive weapon. A belt is something we wear to guard against an attack, while a sword is used to slaughter the enemy. You use the belt of truth (God's Word) to guard against the enemy's deception (lies) he sends our way, while we use the sword of the Spirit (also God's Word) to tear down existing strongholds (deception that took hold) in our minds.

In Romans 12:2 (NKJV), we are told to "be not conformed to this world: but be ye transformed by the renewing of your mind." *How do we renew our minds?* By getting in God's Word! In Ephesians 5:26 (NKJV), this process is referred to as washing of water by the Word: "That he might sanctify and cleanse it with the washing of water by the word."

There are many weapons the devil uses against someone who loves Jesus. Well, do not forget that our love and commitment toward Jesus is what drives him mad the most! This is one weapon he has used through all ages from the smallest to the biggest person around. Many have lost to this devious scheme of the enemy, but the ones who have won this attack have emerged as champions. The devil will steal, kill, and destroy our blessings just to discourage our walk with God. He wants us to question God's goodness. He will make us jobless, steal our joy, and try to shame us, destroy our children all so that we will deny our God. Believe me, there is no extent the enemy will go to see our heart fail. Throughout the Old Testament and even in the New Testament, you will see how the enemy sows seeds of discouragement in the hearts of God's people, simply causing us to take a detour from our destiny.

I changed my thinking to stop being afraid of what man might think and became more concerned with what God would think. I started to do things God's way; it became my aim to do what was right in his eyes regardless of what people thought. When you face fear, it shrinks. If you do not face it, eventually it consumes you. Fear is the opposite of faith; they compete within you. They are opposing forces. Fear pushes out faith, but likewise faith pushes out fear.

To overcome fear, I had to learn to make the distinction between God's perfect will and his permissive will, which he uses to accomplish his divine purpose for my life. God's perfect will is unchangeable. It is with his permissive will, or the various things that he allows into our lives, that we must wrestle before him. It is our reaction to these things allowed by his permissive will that enables us to come and see his perfect will for us. God's permissive will is the testing he uses to reveal his true sons and daughters.

"We know that all things work together for good to those who love God" (Rom. 8:28, NKJV). Do not be afraid to wrestle before God with things that contradict his words. Put up a glorious fight, and you will find yourself empowered with his strength.

As Matthew 6:25–31 (NKJV) says,

> Therefore, I tell you, do not worry about your life, what you will eat or drink: or about your body, or what you will wear. Is not life more important than food, and the body more important than clothes? Look at the birds of the air, they do not sow or reap or store away in barns, and yet your heavenly father feeds them. Are you not much more valuable than they? Who of you by worrying can add a single hour to his life? And why do you worry about clothes? See how the lilies of the field grow. They do not labour or spin. Yet I tell you that not even Solomon in all his splendour was dressed like one of these. If that is how God clothes the grass of the field, which is here today and tomorrow is thrown into the fire, will he not much more clothe you, O ye of little faith? So do not worry, saying, "What shall we eat?" or "What shall we drink?" or "What shall we wear?" For the ungodly run after all these things, and your heavenly Father knows that you need them. But seek first his kingdom and his righteousness, and all these things will be given to you as well. Therefore, do not worry about tomorrow, for tomorrow will worry about itself. Each day has enough trouble of its own.

You can decide to let faith rise in you and push out fear. Here are some simple steps that you can take:

1. When you find yourself worried or afraid, stop for a moment and try to identify the specific thing that you are afraid of.
2. Pray immediately about the specific problem. Do not think, "Oh, I must pray about that later." Pray then and there. The moment you pray, the tide of the battle turns.
3. When you have prayed, think to yourself, "I've cast that upon God. Now it's his problem."
4. Declare that you are a victor, not a victim. He that is in you is greater than he that is in the world.
5. Praise God and thank him that he is working in your life and taking care of the problem.
6. Believe that God is dealing with the problem despite how things appear.
7. Resist the spirit of fear in the name of Jesus.
8. Try to keep away from other people who worry or display fear. Remember that one drowning person cannot help another. You will only make each other worse.

9. Monitor what you are putting into your mind through—books, magazines, newspapers, television, and the internet.

10. Focus on all the good things in your life. Think about what you do have, not what you do not have. There is always some good to be found.

11. Count your blessings, and be thankful. Develop an attitude of gratitude.

12. Do not allow fear to immobilize you. It will shrink if you face it. Say out loud, "I will not fear."

13. Read the scriptures in the Bible that promise protection and help. Meditate on them, and speak them out loud.

14. Declare, "No, devil, you shall not kill, steal, and destroy my life. Jesus came to give me an abundant life, and I believe and receive it."

Scriptures for Encouragement: Psalm 91, 2 Timothy 1:7, Proverbs 3:25–26, Psalm 31:19–20, Psalm 32:8, Hebrews 13:5–6, 1 John 4:4, John 10:10, and 1 John 4:18 (NKJV).

Who Has Bewitched You?

"O foolish Galatians! Who has bewitched you that you should not obey the truth before whose eyes Jesus Christ was clearly portrayed among you as crucified" (Gal. 3:1, NKJV). Paul deals with something we call legalism in the book of Galatians. The Galatians had been wonderfully saved through Paul's preaching, and they were so grateful at that time that he wrote the following: "And my trial which was in my flesh you did not despise or reject, but you received me as an angel of God, even as Christ Jesus" (Gal. 4:14, NKJV).

But something happened to the Galatians. In short, they began to bring the old rules and traditions of Judaism into their new faith and began counting on those rules for part of their salvation. This is why Paul admonishes them by saying, "I marvel that you are turning away so soon from Him who called you in the grace of Christ, to a different gospel" (Gal. 1:6, NKJV). "Are you so foolish? Having begun in the Spirit, are you now being made perfect by the flesh?" (Gal. 3:3, NKJV).

The seriousness of their mistake. It is the same way for many of us today, bewitched by traditions, legalism, and false teaching to the point that we cannot not trust in the truth, before whose eyes Jesus Christ has been evidently set forth, crucified among us. Like the Galatians, we must press hard with questions to put us back in touch with our own experience of God. Questions are the way to start breaking the grip of illusions.

Perception of the truth and how we choose to believe about what is happening to us at any given moment can stop us from having our dreams. We place our own filter (called our belief system) on the truth, and from this create our external reality (through our behaviors) to support this perception. Whether it is true or false, our thinking will make it so. If you have a belief that you are not good enough and therefore not worthy or deserving of your dreams, then anytime you begin to pursue your dreams at some stage in the process, you will always sabotage the outcome because of your underlying belief(s). These beliefs may be very old, and you may not even be aware of them, but if you are not achieving all that you want in your life, then it is highly likely there is a belief pattern(s) holding you back.

We have allowed "the cares of the world" to enter in Matthew 13:22 (NKJV) while forgetting the "much more" of our Heavenly Father. *Did Jesus Christ lie to us?* "Look at the birds of the air" (Matt. 6:26, NKJV); their function is to obey the instincts that God placed within them, and God watches over them. Jesus said if we have the right relationship with him and will obey his Spirit within us, then God will care for our "feathers" too; *He promises.* If we are not, it is because we are not obeying the life God has given us and have cluttered our minds with confusing thoughts and worries.

A warning that needs to be repeated is that "the cares of the world and the deceitfulness of the riches" and the lust of other things will choke out the life of God in us. We constantly condemn ourselves for our past mistakes, even when God's Word makes it plain to us: "Therefore, there is now no condemnation for those who are in Christ Jesus. For the law of the Spirit of life in Christ Jesus has set you free from the law of sin and of death" (Rom. 8:1, NKJV).

Paul in this scripture encourages us that we need not fear condemnation because we can come to God as our loving, forgiving Father (Rom. 8:15–16, NKJV). We who live in shame and guilt over past failures are needlessly condemning ourselves when we ought to be "forgetting what is behind and straining toward what is ahead" (Phil. 3:13, NKJV). Worth repeating again, fear can be paralyzing, "but perfect love drives out fear" (1 John 4:18, NKJV).

As believers, we must understand that our justification is found in Christ alone, in his finished work on the cross, not in what we do or do not do (Rom. 3:28, NKJV). Nothing can separate us "from the love of God that is in Christ Jesus" (Rom. 8:39, NKJV).

My Closeness to God

One of the first things I learned was that my closeness to God is not determined by my situation; it is only determined by revelation, and how much God reveals to me determines how close I am to him. My intellect will never get that; he must put that in my spirit. When I finally figured out through his revelation who I am and what I have, my struggles were not over but manageable. If I am going to walk in my purpose, something must die, namely, my plans.

When God puts his hands on someone and chooses them for his purpose, he will do anything to sustain his choice. I cannot have the pleasure of the world and the power of God; something must die. *So when did my relationship with Jesus Christ change?* I asked the Lord to take me back to the place or event when my trust, confidence, and love in him began to change. As he pursued to take me on this journey of rediscovering who he is and what he means to me, he reminded me what he said to Philip in John 14:9 (NKJV): "Have I been with you so long, and yet you have not known Me, Philip?" These words were not spoken as a rebuke; Jesus was encouraging Philip to draw closer, and that is what Jesus needs from me and from you, to draw closer to him. If I were close to Jesus as I thought I was, I would not believe the lies of my adversaries. I would have stand on his word and his covenant blessings.

What do you mean, Lord? I have an intimate relationship with you; you give me power to cast out demons, to bring about revival, to raise the dead. You even took me back to heaven. And as wonderful and profound those experiences are, Jesus is saying there is a much closer intimacy to come, Maurine. I have called you "friend." Most of us, including myself, do receive his blessings and know his word, but we really do not know him. And because we never knew him, we never received the gifts he gave so freely to us, namely, his life.

Just about now you are saying, well, that is just not me. And I would say it is exactly you. Look honestly at your life. You say you believe Jesus died for you, and in return, he gave you so much that you can experience a victorious life on this earth. Are you living the victorious life he sacrificed himself that you may have? Or is your life filled with shame, disappointments, denial, defeat, uncertainties, sickness, doubt, and the root of them all, unbelief? Whenever we choose not to believe God, we continue to persecute him all over again. Whenever we are obstinate and self-willed and set on our own ambitions, we are hurting Jesus.

God does not want our interactions with him to end at salvation; that is where they begin. If we communicate with him only on a surface level, we cheat ourselves and hinder fulfillment of the Lord's ultimate goal for us, an intimate relationship with him. We are not saved only to be instruments for God but also to be his sons and daughters. He does not turn us into spiritual agents but into spiritual messengers, and the message must be part of us. This is his desire for each of his children.

Many believers unfortunately do not live in the close fellowship that he has made available to us. It is always a joy to Jesus when we walk more intimately with him. It is during that time our beliefs are high, and our lives follow. As his children, our lives must be a holy example of the reality of our message. Even an unsaved person if called will serve, but it takes a heart broken by conviction of sin baptized by the Holy Spirit and crushed into submission to God's purpose to make a person's life a holy example of God's message. God takes us beyond our own aspiration and idea for our lives and molds and shapes us for his purpose.

The purpose of Pentecost was not to teach the disciples something but to make them the incarnation of what they preached so that they would literally become God's message in the flesh. "You shall be witnesses to Me" (Acts 1:8, NKJV).

We must allow God to have complete liberty in our lives before God's message can liberate other people. His liberation must first be real in us, yet many believers can be saved and eternally secure yet relationally distant from the Lord. Some show little or no interest in spiritual things and are unaware of the shallowness of their interactions with God. Others are confused and frustrated, wondering why they do not hear his voice or feel his presence. Even though they attend church, read their Bibles, and pray, he still seems to be far away and disconnected from them.

I know, for a while, I used to be one of those Christians. Our closeness with God will bring us in contact with his nature, and the nature of God will shape our understanding of his call for us and will help us realize what we truly desire to do for him. The call of God is the expression of God's nature, not ours, and we can only recognize the call if that same nature is in us.

The service, which results in my life, is suited to me and is an expression of my nature. Service to God is a wonderful thing; it is the overflow that pours from a life with love and devotion, but there is no call to that. Service is what I bring to the relationship and is the reflection of my identification with the nature of God, and out of devotion to him, service becomes my everyday way of life.

What Does Love Have to Do with This?

Here are some questions to think about: *Did you develop a relationship with God for yourself, or does your knowledge of him come from someone else? Do you love God because you were told to love him? And if you say yes, why do you love him?* One of the profound things I discovered about God is this: he never asks us to do something that he does not first provide for us. "For God loved the world so much that he gave his one and only Son, so that everyone who believes in him will not perish but have eternal life" (John 3:16, NKJV). He uses himself to show us what love is and the ultimate sacrifice that comes with true love. Then he asks us to love him with all our heart and love our neighbors as ourselves.

True love always requires sacrifice, which is why it is so difficult for many of us to love freely and unconditionally. The price to love, as God requires, is sometimes too much for many of us to pay. Love has everything to do with who I am and where I am today. I have done foolish things and made many mistakes since I have been saved, yet God has loved me through them all. It is the love in the mix of my uncertainty that gives me peace, it is the love that comforts me when I am not sure of myself, and it is love that fights for my very soul and sets me free. It is love that heals me through my dysfunctions; it is love that pulls me back when I go too far. God loves me so much through my weakness; he loves me so much through my afflictions; he loves me so much during the time when I did not love him.

This type of love is so amazing it demands my life, it demands my sacrifice, and it demands my all. This type of love man cannot give to me, but when I get ahold of this love, it changes everything. It is a gift from God to humanity. Get ahold of it and receive it. I call it grace. God's grace pours out love, kindness, favor to all who will trust him. We do not have to earn it; we must be in a relationship with him to receive his grace.

What is grace? It is that quality in the heart of God that causes him not to deal with me according to my sins or to retaliate against me according to my iniquities. It is God's faithfulness to me, even when I am not faithful. In fact, it is what love must always be when it meets the unlovely, the weak, the inadequate, the undeserving, and the despicable. It is what author Joseph Cook describes, "Grace is nothing more nor less than the face that love wears when it meets imperfection, weakness, failure, sin." It is God willing to respond to my needs and your needs without reference to merit. It is an unmerited favor. No other person can ever know me as God does. That is why no other person can love me as he can.

God stands willing and able to fashion me into the likeness of the Man Christ Jesus who loves me. This is an offer with no strings attached. This is an offer with no prior commitments exacted. This is an offer with no penalties for failures incurred while trying; thus, the future is secure. Oh, to be sure, it will be different; I can count on that, for this future will be a partnership with my Lord. I need never again feel estranged. I need never again feel alienated. I need never again walk alone in this world. God, who is the unlying God, the unfalse one, guarantees it. He is never false, even though I should prove faithless. He will never let me down, even though I may renounce him (2 Tim. 2:13; Titus 1:2, NKJV). His loving kindness is greater than life, and he is worthy of my praise no matter what season I am in.

The best and dearest of God's saints and servants like myself have found our lot cast in the wilderness, which speak to our lonely and solitary, desolate and afflicted, wanting, wandering, and unsettled, and quite at a loss with what to do with ourselves. On our own, we are not able, but with the love and strength of Jesus, we are able to do all things! Look closely: joy, peace, generosity, faithfulness, **self**-control. Who better to show us the way through all our trials than the Lord who first went through them for us? In many and varied ways, we never even have approached, and for what reason did he do this? For love! His love for us exampled to us every day the way we are to be toward one another.

In Psalm 63 (NKJV), David's song in the wilderness displays David's love for God in a dry, thirsty, and hard place. In a place where the soul is either destroyed or developed, David's soul deepened with the heat of the circumstance. The natural wilderness David was in was also a spiritual wilderness for David. He was in a lonely, solitary, desolate, unsettled, and afflicted place. It was a time with little direction as to what to do, but David found a touch of God for his soul while in the wilderness.

There was no desert in David's heart, though there was a desert around him. We, too, may expect to be cast into rough places here we go hence. In such seasons, but even then, it is our duty and interest to keep up a cheerful communion with God and, like David, discover the benefits of going through our wilderness experiences with God. No one likes to go through this experience of afflictions, but I have come to realize that it is during my wilderness experiences that I have come to know God in ways I did not before. It is the place where I remember God's words of assurance. The only way I could remove the fear from my life is to listen to God's assurance to me.

Yearning for God. The most obvious element in this Psalm is a thirsting and yearning for the Lord (v. 1). Every other pursuit in life seems like a dry desert when compared with the fulfillment of an intimate relationship with God. Our souls and spirits will never experience satisfaction until we discover the joy of devotion to the only one who can fill our emptiness (v. 5). David's passion even had a physical element to it: "my flesh yearns for You" (v. 1). At times, those who have a particularly close connection with the Lord experience an aching for more of him.

Awakened Spiritual Senses. The second aspect of David's deep association with God is his ability to see him (v. 2). One of the results of such closeness is the awakening of our spiritual senses. In learning to know him more deeply, we "see" the one who is unseen. Our understanding of his nature and ways increases dramatically, the scriptures come alive with meaning, and a new sense of discernment guards our minds. Along with this spiritual sensitivity comes the distinct knowledge that it is all from the Lord and not from us.

Satisfaction and Fulfillment. He captures our thoughts and emotions (v. 5–6). Do you remember what it feels like to be in love? No one had to tell you to think about your loved one; your thoughts just automatically flew to him or her. That is what it's like when we love the Savior. The joy of being in his presence satisfies us as nothing else can.

Trust and Dependence. God becomes our shelter in life's storms when we crawl under his wings of protection and cling to him in total dependence (v. 7–8). Those who know intimacy with him feel the safety that comes with submission to his will. Since they know his heart and trust his goodness and wisdom, they have no cause for fear.

Shared Interests. If we are going to grow in oneness with God, we must learn to share his interests. He is always attentive to our concerns, *but do we really care about his desires and purposes? Are you more interested in the Lord or in what he can give you?* Self-focused prayers, neglect of his word, and overly busy schedules send an unspoken message to him: "I'm not interested in you!" If your relationship with the Lord seems stagnant, maybe you have drifted into a self-centered focus that is hindering your friendship with him.

Transformation. No one can have an intimate relationship with God and remain unchanged. A "Sunday Christian" lifestyle will no longer satisfy. As we begin to understand who he is, our love for him grows and motivates us to radical obedience. Our experiences with him teach us that he is faithful and can be trusted. Recognition of the wisdom and goodness of his plans prompts willing submission to his leadership. And before long, time spent with him becomes the best part of each day. Instead of watching the clock, we will want to stay longer because his presence satisfies our souls as nothing else can.

Influence. This kind of passion for the Lord is contagious and influences others. Before I knew God for myself, women and men who knew God intimately always inspired me. As they talk about the things that Christ had done in their lives, a desire to know the Lord like that captured my heart and shaped the direction of my life. It did not happen overnight, but today the most powerful and awesome experience I have is getting in the presence of God, sensing the oneness between his Spirit and mine.

As humans, we have many imperfections that get between God's word of assurance and our own words and thoughts. When we are facing difficulties, the difficulties become like giants, we realized how feeble we are, and God seems to be nonexistent. But remember God's assurance to us: "I will never forsake you." This does not mean I will not be tempted to fear, but I will remember God's words of assurance and his love for me.

Transformation through My Suffering

Why did I have to experience what I had to experience? Through my suffering and brokenness, God transforms me so that I can help someone in their transformation through their suffering. Paul stated in Romans 5:3–4 (NKJV), "Not only so, but we also glory in our sufferings, because we know that suffering produces perseverance; perseverance, character; and character, hope." We learn here that rejoicing is not put on a happy face; instead, he said to rejoice when we suffer. He taught that God could transform our lives through our suffering. He is the still small voice that whispers to us to trust him. He is the light within our darkness penetrating through our bewilderment.

So why did I have to go through so many painful experiences to get to the place where I could surrender all to God? Romans 6:6 (NKJV) says something interesting about the "old man. It says, "Knowing this, that our old man is crucified with him, that the body of sin might be destroyed, that henceforth we should not serve sin." The first part of this verse is important to know because it tells us that if you have been saved by Jesus, the "old man" was crucified and put to death with Jesus on the cross, at least from the standpoint of its judicial standing before God. Sin has been punished. Our sins, all our sins, have been punished through Christ on the cross. Your old man, our sinful nature was hanging there symbolically in the person of Christ. Oh, what a great salvation he has given to us.

What a wonderful future we have in heaven because of Christ. But heaven has not come yet. We are still in this world, and we must learn some important things about living for Christ in this world. In this part of Ephesians 4 (NKJV), we are being told some important principles regarding having a new life now that we have come to Christ. We are supposed to be different from the unbelievers around us. *What are the principles involved that allow us to be different in the right ways?* But regarding the practical reality of my day-to-day life, I decided, regarding the old man and the new, one or the other will control my life each day; one or the other will control my response to any situation. I cannot say that I am going to serve God in some things but not in others.

This all-or-nothing principle is expressed in several different ways in the New Testament. For example, Jesus said to the church at Laodicea in Revelation 3:16 (KJV), "So then because thou art lukewarm, and neither cold nor hot: I will spue thee out of my mouth." The apostle Paul spoke of his own life of following Christ, and he said, "I die daily." *In what way did he die?* He died to his own selfish desires, but notice that it was not something that happened one time forever. This dying to the old man and my desires must take place repeatedly because the old man is still there, waiting to take control should I allow him to do so.

God will for me as his child is to have life and have it more abundantly, but if there is war going on within me, then I cannot see or experience the manifestation of God's covenant blessings and promises in my life. We all have human bodies that were exercised in sin before we came to Christ. Now we are being exercised in righteousness by the Holy Spirit. Change does not often come instantly or easily. It takes diligent obedience over a period of time to see our bodies brought under the control of the Spirit in all areas.

Thus, in Colossians 2:6–10 (NKJV), Paul admonishes us to "put off the old man with his deeds" and "put on the new man who is renewed." To the Colossians, he explains that since we have put off the old man and have put on the new man. We should not let the deeds of the old man manifest themselves but instead put on the deeds of the new man. His basis of appeal for new conduct is that a believer is a new creation in Christ Jesus. The believer has a grace he did not have before because of his standing in Christ Jesus.

The process of patience, which we eventually learned during our suffering, is internally driven. Our confidence is used to create a mental image of how things could be in our circumstances. Suffering, in contrast, is propelling almost entirely by influences from the external world. Instead of being drawn toward the new me, I am kicked out of the old. And my idols are not belittled. Rather, they are smashed to pieces right in front of my eyes. If this sounds like a painful process, it is. So now that we have this point settled, let us look at the details.

Do you remember when you were a kid, and your parents wanted you to do something that was good for you, but you did not want to comply, you want to be rebellious about it? Do you remember this saying: "You will come whether you like it or not"? "You can decide whether you want to cooperate or whether I will have to drag you kicking and screaming." Obviously we are going to have a lot less misery if we go along willingly.

That is pretty much how it was with God and me. He had to kick the old man out through my suffering. In practical terms, my experiences with suffering allow me to understand my situation after I have gone through it. Looking back, I was able to see a logical progression. While suffering, though, I cannot see the logical reason for my predicament because I lack the perceived confidence to apply logical thinking, which is in contrast to how I learned through patience. When I am patient, I understand what I am going through while it is happening, though I may only comprehend it one step at a time. Because it is not emotionally driven as my suffering is, it is based on revelation knowledge, which brings forth patience, and patience has its perfect works.

In suffering, the *external world* creates a separation between me and not me. That which is me must be *worse* than that which is not. This then put emotional pressure on my thought to abandon the old me. Unless my personal experiences are in some way unpleasant, I will not want to leave them. Similarly, unless others are in a better situation, I will not know that things could be different. Therefore, I must experience some sort of personal "failure" from the external world, something that I *cannot* ignore. How awful must it be? Bad enough to get my attention and hold it. Unless this disaster forces me to admit that I am in an awful predicament, it will not be enough. When relative suffering fails to motivate change in my life, then growth can only be achieved through *imposed* suffering. Anything less I will either ignore or reject it.

The battle is in our mind; therefore, suffering, which is *externally* driven, *indirectly* promotes personal transformation by dragging the mind through the steps of personal transformation. First, I must face the unpleasant facts about my situation, and then I must figure how to live with this unpleasantness while trying to find the perceiving energy to continue within the judging of my predicament. Finally, the trauma changes my way of life; I can no longer continue with my present actions. After going through all that, I realize that I have been changed *inside*. I am no longer the same person that I was; no longer can I even conceive of living as I did before.

"If any man be in Christ, he is a new creation; old things are passed away; all things are become new." The reason that all things are called new is because now I have a new man in addition to the old man. The old man is represented by the deceitful lusts, by the strong selfish desires that every human being has and has had such as adultery, fornication, uncleanness, lasciviousness, idolatry, witchcraft, hatred, variance, emulations, wrath, strife, seditions, and heresies. *In contrast to the strong selfish desires of the old man, the new man does away with those desires by being centered on Christ and by being surrendered to Christ's will, bearing the fruit of the spirit, which is love, peace, long suffering, gentleness, goodness, faith, meekness, and temperance.* Either I will surrender to my selfishness, or I will surrender to Christ.

When I talk about spiritual choices and the renewing of the mind, I am also talking about behaviors that result from those choices and from those thoughts. And so verse 25 starts listing some very practical things that will result if someone has put off the old man. Another way of looking at it is this: we make choices concerning each action that we take in each circumstance. In each one of those circumstances, either we choose what the old man would do, or we choose what the new man would do.

Notice what Ephesians 4:28 (KJV) says that you should do with your income once you have work that meets your needs. It says, "That he may have to give to him that needeth." The believer who is living according to the new man thinks of others. Remember, the old man is selfish; the new man is generous and kind and compassionate. If you have true compassion, then when you see your brother in need, you will not shut up your bowels of compassion from him, but you will give of your substance to ease his need. That tells you right there what God wants you to use some of your abundance for, to help human beings who have physical needs. You are a spiritual person if you care about the physical needs of others. This is God's plan for the spiritual person: you work, you gain, you use some of your gain for your own needs, and you use some of your gain for the needs of others. That is what God does; he helps us both physically and spiritually. Every good thing that we have comes from God who is the giver of all good things. God gave his Son to die on a cruel cross so that we could be saved from our sins.

Before I became enlightened about my suffering, I would blame my image of "God" for my personal suffering, which means I did not have to change. Without suffering, we cannot grow. Without suffering, we cannot get the peace and joy we deserve. Please do not run away from your suffering; embrace it and cherish it. Go to the God your Father, sit with him, and show him your pain. He who knows the beginning from the end, he will look at you with loving kindness, compassion, and mindfulness and show you ways to embrace your suffering and look deeply into it. With his love, mercy, and grace, you will be able to heal the wounds in your heart and the wounds in the world. Our suffering is never in vain; it has the capacity of showing us the path to freedom in Jesus Christ. Embrace your suffering, and let it reveal to you the way to peace, and like David, our souls may deepen with the heat of our circumstances.

How Does the New Man Reign in Our Lives When the Old Man Is Always with Us?

In short, died to self, have that white funeral. Until we die to our preconceived ideas, traditions, perception, habits, and religion, our mind will always battle against our will. *Which man will rule each day?* Here is a hint: whichever has the most space in our hearts will win every time. This process of letting go is the most difficult for most people, no matter how saintly they think they are. I have been through this myself, and I have no doubt this is why God uses these methods of allowing my struggles to make me break bread and pour out wine. It is through this process that I have come to trust him in all areas of my life to the point of surrender all. That allows me to develop a deeper, more intimate relationship of trust, respect, honor, and love like I have never experienced—in some cases, a coequal partner with Jesus Christ that I have ever known before.

This is what Jesus Christ meant when he said, "But I call you Friend," which is an amazing statement for me to make, considering the enormous number of supernatural encounters I experience with God. This goes back to my foundational point, experiences are great parts of our spiritual and physical development, but our experiences are attached to our emotions, and our emotions are at times unstable. So if our faith is based on our experiences only and not revelation knowledge from God, we will be like the church of the Laodiceans in Revelation 3:16 (KJV): "So then because thou art lukewarm, and neither cold nor hot: I will spue thee out of my mouth."

When I speak of coequal partners, I do not mean I am equal to God. God is sovereign and is God all by himself. But I do partner with him in the areas of my life that he calls me to do, like writing this book as well as the book I wrote before this one and the humanitarian organization that I am responsible for. My name is on the book, but I have recognized from the beginning that I do not have the knowledge or the forfeiture to write books like these. The knowledge and the wisdom it takes are well beyond my paygrade. God calling also pertains to where he is calling me from and what must he do to pull certain things out of me to get me to where he is calling me to. I am humbled and honored that he is taking me step by step through the process of rediscovering who he is on a level that I am now ready to receive.

So after all this time, how does the new man that Jesus Christ died on the cross so that he may reign in my life take its place? I first must crucify the old man every day. *How do I do this?* I look in the mirror at the reflection of Jesus Christ, and I take my cues from him, which means if the choices I must make each day are not consistent with the teachings of Jesus Christ, then I have to make a decision. Either I will choose what the old man would do, or I will choose what the new man would do. That means I will have to give up some, if not all, ideas of the world system of solving problems. Giving up my own selfish desires, I may have to give up some friends and sometimes relatives. It means that I may be ridiculed by others for my decisions concerning my beliefs.

This walk of being a "witness" for Christ is not an easy one, but there is nothing else on this earth that will give you the peace, joy, satisfaction, and fulfillment like being a disciple of Jesus Christ.

I received a revelation from God recently that put everything in perspective for me. I was preparing for my morning worship with my late friend, Teresa Lucas, who had been going through her own wilderness experiences. As I was getting prepared to call her, I decided to go through my daily reading from *My Utmost for His Highest* to see if there was something God had to say to me through the pages. The subject at hand was "Taking the Initiative Against Depression," and the teaching was taken from 1 Kings 19:5 (NKJV). Now I have been through many wilderness experiences in my life. In fact, I am going through a few right now. I always knew that God allowed or engineered my circumstances to teach me whatever lessons I needed to learn at the time, or worse yet, the devil had devised a trap for me. And it's true that there are times, as discussed earlier, when God does allow situations in our lives to teach us how to trust him more, to prepare us for the next level or place in our lives he is positioning us for. In fact, Deuteronomy 8:2–18 (NKJV) is a perfect example of why God would lead us into the wilderness:

Remember the LORD, Your God

Every commandment which I command you today you must be careful to observe, that you may live and multiply, and go in and possess the land of which the LORD swore to your fathers. And you shall remember that the LORD your God led you all the way these forty years in the wilderness, to humble you and test you, to know what was in your heart, whether you would keep His commandments or not. So He humbled you, allowed you to hunger, and fed you with manna which you did not know nor did your fathers know, that He might make you know that man shall not live by bread alone; but man lives by every word that proceeds from the mouth of the LORD. Your garments did not wear out on you, nor did your foot swell these forty years. You should know in your heart that as a man chastens his son, so the LORD your God chastens you.

Therefore you shall keep the commandments of the LORD your God, to walk in His ways and to fear Him. For the LORD your God is bringing you into a good land, a land of brooks of water, of fountains and springs, that flow out of valleys and hills; a land of wheat and barley, of vines and fig trees and pomegranates, a land of olive oil and honey; a land in which you will eat bread without scarcity, in which you will lack nothing; a land whose stones are iron and out of whose hills you can dig copper. When you have eaten and are full, then you shall bless the LORD your God for the good land, which He has given you. Beware that you do not forget the LORD your God by not keeping His commandments, His judgments, and His statutes which I command you today, lest when you have eaten and are full, and have built beautiful houses and dwell in them; and when your herds and your flocks multiply, and your silver and your gold are multiplied, and all that you have is multiplied; when your heart is lifted up, and you forget the LORD your God who brought you out of the land of Egypt, from the house of bondage; who led you through that great and terrible wilderness, in which were fiery serpents and scorpions and thirsty land where there was no water; who brought water for you out of the flinty rock; who fed you in the wilderness with manna, which your fathers did not know, that He might humble you and that He might test you, to do you good in the end then you say in your heart, "My power and the might of my hand have gained me this wealth." And you shall remember the LORD your God, for it is He who gives you power to get wealth, that He may establish His covenant which He swore to your fathers, as it is this day. Then it shall be, if you by any means forget the LORD your God, and follow other gods, and serve them and worship them, I testify against you this day that you shall surely perish. As the nations which the LORD destroys before you, so you shall perish, because you would not be obedient to the voice of the LORD your God.

What I have found out through 1 King 19:1–15 (NKJV) is that we lead ourselves into most of our wilderness experiences by the way we respond to circumstances we encounter in our daily lives. I know! But get a grip of it; I had to.

Elijah's story brings my own story to life, and if you stay with me, it will bring understanding to your own life experiences that we call the wilderness. First, if we respond to the circumstance in our lives, whatever they might be, with fear, it will always lead us to a wilderness experience. *Why?* Because when we get anxious about a conflict, we always want to help God out as if we can do it better job than he does. We go back to a place of familiarity, a place where we have been before, have had some success and are comfortable. Except this time, your familiar place no longer works. God has shut those doors; you cannot go back.

In 1 Kings 19:2 (NKJV), it is explained how Elijah became fearful of Jezebel when he heard she was going to kill him. Now you would expect Elijah, who was a great prophet of God, to respond differently to this threat, but he did not. Elijah failed in the very point at which he was strongest, and that is where most of us fail. In scripture, it is the wisest man who proves himself to be the greatest fool, just as the meekest man, Moses, spoke hasty and bitter words. Abraham failed in his faith and Job in his patience; so he who was the most courageous of all men fled from an angry woman.

According to 1 Kings 19:4 (NKJV), because of his fears, Elijah himself went a day's journey into the wilderness and came and sat down under a juniper tree, "and he requested for himself that he might die; and said, it is enough now, O Lord, take away my life; for I am not better than my fathers."

When Elijah examined the apparent failure of his work, he instinctively set the blame on his own unworthiness. It was because he was a sinner as the rest of his ancestors that the work seemed to fail. It is usually in the place we expect God to show up and rescue us, but he does not, at least not the way we are expecting to be rescued. Instead he speaks with a soft voice. Thankfully, this was a *prayer not answered* for Elijah. In fact, *Elijah was one of the few men* in the Bible to never die! We can imagine that as he was caught up into heaven, he smiled and thought of this prayer, and the blessed "no" that answered his prayer.

To receive a *no* answer from God can be better than receiving a *yes* answer. What was even more enlightening for me was verses 11 to 12 because God was with Elijah in the wilderness, and the elements still came against him, but when the elements passed, he heard God's voice. God said to Elijah, "Why are you doing here, Elijah?" And it is the same question God is asking us. "Why are you here? Why are you in this mess? You did not have to be here, Maurine. If you only trust me and know that you can do nothing without me because 'it's not my power or my force but by my Spirit,'" said the Lord. Again, God repeated the question, *"What are doing here?"* Then he complained of his discouragement and whether should God's prophets go with their complaints of that kind but to their master. The Lord gave him an answer. He declared that the wicked house of Ahab shall be rooted out and that the people of Israel shall be punished for their sins. He showed that Elijah was not left alone as he had supposed and that a helper should at once be raised up for him. Thus, all his complaints were answered and provided for.

And look what God did in the end to Elijah. He sent him back into the wilderness, where he had placed him in the first place to fulfill his purpose, not the wilderness that Elijah created for himself because of his fears. And we, too, must learn to stay in the place where God places us, even when it becomes difficult and it seems like nothing is happening, is changing, or is moving fast enough for us. This is the time the adversary takes the opportunity to further push us into our created wilderness place by giving us thoughts, ideas, and suggestions that are contrary to God's Words.

In verse 4, Elijah said, "It is enough," yet it was not enough, even for his own enjoyment, for the Lord had more blessings in store for him. It was so with Elijah, for he was to have that wonderful revelation of God on Mount Horeb. He had more to enjoy, and the later life of Elijah appears to have been one of calm communion with his God; he seems never to have had another fainting fit, but to the end, his sun shone brightly without a cloud. So it was not enough; how could he know that it was? It is God alone who knows when we have done enough and enjoyed enough, but we do not know.

It is important to note that the motivation for God entering a communion with Elijah was to correct Elijah's false perception that led to fear. Prior to forming that connection, he commanded Elijah to eat, thereby ministering to his physical weakness. Both the spirit and the body need to be fed. A child of God who is experiencing depression must receive spiritual as well as physical healing. It is important as believers who seek to help them that we understand their need for both. It was very gracious for God to deal with his servant in this way. We might have expected rebuke or remonstrance or chastisement, but we would hardly have expected such loving, gentle treatment as this.

God set Elijah on a two-hundred-mile, forty-day trip to Mount Horeb, also known as Mount Sinai. This shows that God did not demand an immediate recovery from Elijah. He allowed the prophet time to recover from his spiritual depression. How precious is God's loving kindness toward us?

We can, in the present, have the victorious living that God's Word promises if we just believe and receive what God said about us and what we can have. It is difficult for our adversary to fool us when we know the truth of who we are in Christ. We are the offspring of God; we are made in his own imagine. We are anointed for the call, we have the wisdom of God, we have the gift and the fruit of the spirit, but because we do not know these truths, we reject them. That is what 1 Peter 2:2 (KJV) is saying: "As newborn babies desire the sincere milk of the world that ye may grow thereby." But as the physical babe cannot grow into adulthood on milk alone, neither can "spiritual babes" grow into men and women of God solely on "the milk of the Word." There must come a time when the babe begins to assimilate solid food or "meat." We must be strong in the Word of God.

The apostle Paul wrote to the Corinthian believers and reminded them that he "determined not to know anything among them, save Jesus Christ and Him crucified" (1 Cor. 2:2, NKJV). This was all they could understand at the time because of their carnality. He continues in 1 Corinthians 3:1–4 (NKJV) from these scriptures that it is evident that "being satisfied with the simple things" is a mark of carnality. Without a doubt, this carnal attitude has contributed largely to the widespread illiteracy in biblical knowledge among God's people in our day. Instead of being men and women of God, many of us are still "children, tossed to and fro and carried about with every wind of doctrine!" (Eph. 4:14).

Peter and Paul are both right, but today there is something else that we need to keep in mind, and that is we have had church traditions for almost two thousand years. These church traditions are based mostly on the kingdom gospel, not the grace gospel. Apostle Paul said some would pervert the Gospel of Christ. How did they do it in Paul's day? It appears to me that they turned from Paul's grace gospel to follow James and the kingdom gospel mixed with the law. This is falling from grace. Galatians 5:4 (KJV) says, "Christ is become of no effect unto you, whosoever of you is justified by the law; ye are fallen from grace." Faith for us should be like money. The more we have, the more we can do. That is why God wants us to have great faith. We need to receive the promise through faith that Jesus Christ paid in full at the cross. His sacrifice for us on the cross was complete and settles our account. If we do not believe what grace provides, then grace does not apply. I do not deserve it, but God puts it in my hand because I believe.

Grace has called us to operate outside our human abilities, so if we are not tapping into the grace of God, we cannot make it. We must learn to abound in the grace God gives us, which means we give according to the level that God has made the provision for us. Our giving should not be motivated for us to be blessed because we are already blessed. We need to examine the purpose of our giving; unwilling hearts will not allow us to tap into that grace supply (2 Cor. 9:8, NKJV). God loves a cheerful giver. God already positions us for a lifestyle of miracles. Every need we have is already supplied in the spiritual, and we must just believe by faith to receive it in our natural life. We need to eat the Word of God, which means to spend time in the word, meditate on it, let the Holy Spirit bear witness, and bring forth that in which we believe.

MAURINE MCFARLANE

Prayer to Defeat Fear

Dear Heavenly Father,

you have not given me a spirit of fear

but a spirit of a conqueror. I will say of the Lord

you are my refuge and my fortress, my God; in you will I trust.

I will boldly confront my adversary because you are my confidence.

Mine eyes are ever toward you, Lord, for you shall puck my feet out of the net.

Remember, O Lord, thy tender mercies and thy loving kindness,

for they have been ever of old. Look upon my affliction and my pain,

and forgive all my sins. You are my light and my salvation.

I will not be afraid when life overwhelms me.

I will not be afraid to fail.

I will not be afraid to succeed.

I will not be afraid of change.

I will not be afraid of the giant I created in my mind

because you are my God, and I trust you to lead me.

O how great is thy goodness, which thou hast laid

up for them that love thee, in Jesus's name,

Amen.

CHAPTER FIFTEEN

A STATE OF PARALYSIS

It is Sunday, February 23, 2014, two years after I started this book. It has taken me this long to get here; frankly, I had no idea what "here" was until this moment. Three days ago, I thought the last chapter would be fifteen but with a different subheading, "The Manifestations." I was planning to put this book aside for several more months, if not years, not sure how long God would take to manifest his promises in my life. After all, for the book to end, some things must be manifested in my life that I have prayed and believe God for, or this book would be a lie.

So why the extra chapters, and what about the subtitle, "A State of Paralysis"? What does God mean by that? I look quite healthy. Looking at myself in the mirror, everything appears to be in order. I do need to lose some weight, but nothing is broken that I can see. I acknowledge I have been in the valley now for many years, but for the past three years, it has been more severe. Some of the challenges in my life on the surface seem to have no end. Every turn I take is another block, another disappointment, but I am still pushing and navigating my way through. I admit it would be easy for me to go through my valley experiences if I only had myself to contend with, but when God allows other people to become part of my experiences, it is when it really gets tough.

God has placed in my heart a great love and compassion for humanity, and so when someone becomes part of my valley experiences, I am always trying to save them from going through it. However, the more I try to stop it, the greater the challenges become until I realized it was necessary for that person to have that experience in his or her life. Most of us go through our lives thinking we are fine, life is good, "I am good person," "I give to the poor," "I have it going on," especially if we have some level of what society calls success. God, however, knows the beginning from the end. He sees our hearts, not just the external part that the world can see and glorified. When he is ready to show us who we really are and what is really in us, he will allow events and circumstances in our lives to expose what we have been trying to hide from others and from ourselves.

And as much as I would like to prevent the other person from experiencing the same pain I am experiencing, it is also unjust for me to stop what God is trying to do in that person's life, no matter how painful it is. God is always trying to make us better than we are, more powerful than we think we are, and like great wine, we, too, must go through the press until every bitter taste in us is forced out so the best of us can come forth. What does this have to do with paralysis? Hang with me a little while longer, and I will show you as it has been revealed to me.

What Is Paralysis?

To have a greater understanding of what God was saying to me, I did some research on what it means to be paralyzed. I have some ideas of what it means, but I wanted the professional to explain it to me, and this is what I came away with. The muscle is a special kind of tissue that enables our bodies to move. It is under the control of the nervous system, which processes messages to and from all parts of the body. Sometimes the nerve cells, or neurons, that control the muscles become diseased or injured. When that happens, a person loses the ability to move the muscles voluntarily, and we say that the person is paralyzed.[1]

Paralysis of the muscles of the face, arm, and leg on one side of the body is called hemiplegia ("hemi" means "half") and usually results from damage to the opposite side of the brain. Damage to the nerves of the spinal cord affects different parts of the body, depending on the amount of damage and where it occurred. Paralysis of both lower limbs is called paraplegia, and paralysis of both arms and both legs is called quadriplegia. Paralysis may be temporary or permanent, depending on the disease or injury. Because paralysis can affect any muscle in the body, a person may lose not only the ability to move but also the ability to talk or to breathe unaided.[1] The word comes from the Greek παράλυσις, meaning "disabling of the nerves," itself from παρά (para), "besides, by" + λύσις (lysis), "loosing," and that from λύω (luō), "to lose."[2]

I went over the definition several times. I now got it as I held my breath. I am utterly amazed with God. His love is greater than life, and he refuses to allow us to stay in a paralyzed state of life, especially when we do not know we are paralyzed. A state of paralysis can be mental or physical; it can affect different parts of our body, our lives, and those who are around us. When we are physically paralyzed, we can see where the problem lies, but when we are paralyzed mentally or spiritually, it is much harder to identify the problem.

The Holy Spirit took me to John 5:1–9 (NKJV), the story about the paralyzed man who stayed at the pool in Bethesda for thirty-eight years because he could not get in the pool. When the angel came down at a certain season and after the trouble of the water, the first person who stepped in was made whole. When Jesus came on the scene, he saw the man lay there and knew he had been there a long time, so Jesus asked the man, "Why are you not whole?" The man told Jesus he had no one to help him in the pool when the water was troubled. He basically said to Jesus, "I have no resources, no money, no opportunity. I had no father growing up or no mother. I have no opportunity." You name it, he did not have it. For thirty-eight years, he settled and developed a climate at the pool of Bethesda with which he was comfortable.

Christ, by asking this question, designs to excite this person's faith, hope, and a greater desire of being healed. Jesus wants the man to reflect on his miserable state, that he might be better prepared to receive a cure and to value it when it comes. Jesus told him to take up the bed and walk, and immediately the man was whole. For the man to change the climate he had grown comfortable in all these years, he had to go to another dimension in his faith to believe Jesus;

he had to want it bad enough to make the effort for his healing. He had to get out of his comfort zone, away from his circle of influence from the climate he had developed over the years.

Despair and discouragement were an inherent part of the place where this story occurs. The dynamic of the story is that a man who had no hope, endlessly reciting the reasons he could not be healed, moved from his own despair and discouragement to being healed suddenly after thirty-eight years of lying in wait at the pool, unable to get into it. What is profound for me about this story, other than how it relates so much to my own life (not all areas of my life, mind you), is that there are areas of my life where I have allowed myself to settle. This is because of what I have told myself about the situation I have made comfortable for me to live with and accepted. The insight for me is how easily we can create the climate we now live in and call it ordinary. And when someone from the outside questions us, we have our excuses rehearsed and ready, not taking any responsibility for our parts in the creation of our circumstances.

Well, how did I get here? Once again, God provides the answer for me through an amazing sermon at church today given by one of our young ministers, the reverend Andrew Grannum of New Covenant Church of Philadelphia. He titles it "climate change." He began by telling a story about taking a trip to Atlantic City with his wife for Valentine's Day weekend, just after a snowstorm had hit Philadelphia. However, the closer they got to the Atlantic Ocean, the less snow they saw until eventually there was no snow in Atlantic City. He said he assumed that because of the closeness in distance to Philadelphia, the weather would be the same. He said the Atlantic City did not have any snow that day, but he noticed and felt the heaviness in the atmosphere, a heaviness he could see on the faces of the people around the hotel. He then asked the congregation the definition of climate change.

Climate Change

Most people know that it is colder on top of a mountain than near the ground, but few know why. And even less know that the *atmosphere* warms up again! Earth's temperature is a balancing act, and Earth's temperature depends on the balance between energy entering and leaving the planet's system. When incoming energy from the sun is absorbed by the Earth system, Earth warms. When the sun's energy is reflected into space, Earth avoids warming. When energy is released back into space, Earth cools. Many factors, both natural and human, can cause changes in Earth's energy balance, including the following[3]:

- Changes in the greenhouse effect, which affects the amount of heat retained by Earth's atmosphere
- Variations in the sun's energy reaching Earth
- Changes in the reflectivity of Earth's atmosphere and surface

Before there can be a climate change, there first must be an atmosphere change. *Why?* Because something must be injected in an atmosphere that produces the change. That change, good or bad, then creates a climate, which then develops into a stronghold. A stronghold is a way of thinking that leads the people in that atmosphere to develop certain behavior and habits. In essence, an atmosphere change occurs because one person cooperates with the spiritual climate. According to the reverend Andrew Grannum, kingdom living is not for the lazy people who are not willing to do what it takes to bring forth change in their lives or the lives of others. To change the climate in our community and our family, we first need to understand that it will be necessary to operate in a different dimension. Simply put, we must operate on a higher thought; we cannot do the same things and expect a different result. Change agents and history makers are people who go beyond themselves to create the change they seek.

So what happened that allowed me to go from being excited about Jesus Christ, walking totally in faith, giving up all that he asked of me to serve him, going to any place he sent me, and making any sacrifice required, to a person whose faith now was lukewarm? What a number the devil did on my mind. Religion, at times, will hinder us from receiving right and believing right what God has for us. Like too many religious people, when things were not happening or going well for me, when the desires of my heart seemed to be denied, I would develop automatic responses for every scenario like "I am waiting on the Lord," "It's not my seasons," "God timing is not my timing." These words keep us paralyzed because they keep us from taking responsibility for our part. I came in agreement with the spiritual atmosphere, and before I knew it, this became a way of thinking.

To make my situation worse, most of the people around me were in the same paralyzed state. We had all developed a climate in our environments that becomes a way of thinking, a stronghold, and our lives is the evidence of that. Broke and disgusted most of the time, struggling to maintain our faith most of the time, and when life challenges confronted us, we failed and flickered. To encourage ourselves, we quote Bible verses we don't really believe in our hearts such as, "I can do all things through Christ Jesus that strengths me" or "I am the head and not the tail." Heaven forbid we could be honest and say, "I am doubtful about what I said I believe" or "My faith has failed me." Instead they always pretend everything is fine. Someone asks, "How are you, Sister Saint?" The usual response is "Blessed and highly favored." *Really? How come my life is a complete mess?*

My ministries had major financial challenges. I seem to be gaining weight every hour, and I cannot stop it. I am in the middle of a lawsuit, a long-held relationship is coming to an end, and everything I put my hands to lately turns to dust, and this is on a good day. Some days I feel as if I am in the twilight zone, and I cannot find my way out. Some call it a wilderness place; in my case, God calls it a state of paralysis. In this state, all other aspects of my life are affected because I have come to accept the status quo. It is easier to accept the new climate change when everyone around me also accepts the changes. It gives me a sense of comfort; after all, I am not the only one in this state. I have company that confirms it.

It is not so bad until Jesus asks me, "Why are you not whole? Why are you in this place, Maurine?" And just like the man at the pool, I, too, gave my Lord many reasons why I was not whole, including blaming him for my state. Thank God for his grace, mercy, and everlasting love for me, he refused to leave me in this state of paralysis. He commanded me to take up my bed and walk. He was basically saying, "Get up and clean up your mess and move on to the life I have predestined for you from the foundation of the earth. Get up and take care of your Father's business."

Frustration

You do understand that if you are in a state of paralysis, then frustration will be a major part of your life. Frustration is described as a feeling of dissatisfaction or discouragement that occurs when an individual's needs, goals, or expectations are not met. It is what I feel when my efforts are being blocked or cannot be achieved. Very often I may experience a range of negative emotions such as anger, resentment, annoyance, and distrust that I projected on God because of my frustration. It took me a long time to understand why God was allowing certain events and people in my life that were obviously keeping me from accomplishing the task he gave me to do. After all, I told myself, "I did everything the Lord told me to do. I have made and continue to make an enormous amount of investments in the Kingdom of God. *So why am I still struggling? Why so many barriers? And how do I get around them?*"

Frustration always leads to downfall and deviation because it wastes precious thinking ability and attention, which otherwise would have been used in constructive or creative work. It is during this state that I made my greatest mistakes—I insisted on doing it myself because God must need my help. After all, there is no movement; things are not progressing as fast as I would like. *How long does God expect me to wait for his promises to manifest in my life?*

Be careful on how you make decisions in this state. You will find yourself taking the opinion of those around you above the instructions God gave to you. Trying to make those around you feel involved and relevant is good; you always want to make your friends, family, and team feel they are part of the big picture. It cannot, however, come at the price of being disobedient to God's instructions. Our surrounding factors, as well as assisting the team, play a major role in our working ability. If our working ability gets hampered by external factors such as noncooperation of workers, that will bring frustration. We cannot expect any improvement against expressed will of other person if one is unwilling to put in the effort for it. If we waste our energy on such futile teammates who, in fact, are not interested in cooperating with us, we get frustrated. We waste precious energy and attention, and we will find ourselves stuck in a downward spiral of performance.

I went to scripture to find out more about a leader whom God called to lead a people out of bondage to the Promised Land. In the end, though, this leader did not make it into the Promised Land because he listened to the people around him instead of the instructions God gave him. Moses was probably one of the greatest Old Testament prophets of God, and he came far short of the destiny that God had intended for him. You will see how his example of failure applies to us. Can it help us avoid repeating his mistake? If we can, we will radically change what we say to whom and when. Many times, it would be better to keep our mouths shut and not say anything than to speak the problem and remain in unbelief and miss out on God's answer to our problems. God told Moses that if he would only speak to the rock, the rock would obey his words. That statement boggles my minds. *God will do what I say?* If we study the Bible and believe what it says about the word and what we speak, we would certainly change many of the things that we say. The problem is that most of us fall into the same unbelief category and continue to speak about our problems.

Why Did Moses Not Enter the Promised Land?

The examples written in the Old Testament are there so that we can learn not to repeat the same mistakes that they made. If we can learn these lessons from Moses, I think we can apply them to our situations today. We have a better covenant, established upon better promises, yet we do not possess them automatically. Even though God had already given the children of Israel the Promised Land, they were required to do something to possess it.

Let us examine what kept Moses out of possessing God's Promised Land. In chapter 20 of Numbers, Moses has a big problem again. He is attempting to lead the people of Israel through a desert. There is little to no water to drink, and the people and the animals are all very thirsty. Moses goes to God, asks for help, and God responds with a set of specific instructions, so let's now start reading what God says to Moses in the desert. For your information, this story is covered with types and shadows of spiritual things to come.

The children of Israel are a type of the church. Moses and Aaron are types of the leaders in the church. The rock is a type of Jesus Christ. The Promised Land is a type of the Word of God, the promises of the New Covenant. The wilderness can represent the time of trials or tests in the life of believers. The water is most often representative of the spiritual drink of God's Word. Numbers 20:8 (NKJV) says, "Take the rod, and gather thou the assembly together, thou, and Aaron thy brother, and speak ye unto the rock before their eyes; and it shall give forth his water, and thou shalt bring forth to them water out of the rock: so, thou shalt give the congregation and their beasts drink."

Now here is the real lesson from the story. I believe that we can see and learn a lot from the next instruction that God gives to Moses. Step 4: God said for the leadership to "speak to the rock." *What did the Bible say was the rock?* The rock represents Jesus Christ. Jesus Christ is the answer to our every problem. *What was Moses's problem? No water or angry, upset rebellious people.* Obviously Moses's problem was his own people. We need to understand this because it is especially important to see. People are the biggest problem in any church, ministry, or organization. People like to talk, gossip, complain, criticize, and do many other ungodly things. People will start divisions, confrontations, and internal fights and just complain about anything that they think does not fit with what they want to see happen. People will start petitions, call for meetings, and try to run the show and all along disregard God's appointed leadership, his anointing, his plans, and his purposes.

God has placed leadership to do a specific job in a specific way. Most of the time, God deals with the leadership and tells them exactly what to do and say to the people. This is a significant learning point from the patterns found in the story of Moses and the children of Israel. God never addressed the congregation or spoke to anyone in the congregation directly about how to run the group or what to do. God always went through his chosen leader, recognizing spiritual organization and structure. God gave Moses a specific set of instructions with a limited number of steps.

These are not complicated steps, but people sometimes hear what they want to hear instead of what God says, and that gets them into trouble in a big way. As we read through the rest of this chapter, we find that Moses did not do what God said to do. Let us carefully examine the specific set of instructions that God gave:

1. Take your rod.
2. Get your brother Aaron.
3. Gather the people before the rock.
4. Speak to the rock.
5. Give everyone a drink.

Moses makes a great start to obeying God but has a lousy ending. Again let us examine what Moses did, according to these two verses, and list the steps he took:

1. Moses took the rod.
2. Moses met with his brother Aaron.
3. Moses and Aaron gathered the people together before the rock.
4. Moses spoke to the people.

The first three steps seem to be perfect matches to the instructions that God gave to Moses. When did God ever tell Moses to say anything to the people? I know that Moses had to say something to them, to gather them or assemble them before the rock. But when did God tell Moses to say to the people after they were all gathered? *Did God tell Moses to preach to the congregation? Did God say to tell the congregation anything at all?* I do not think that he did. This represents the beginning of the downfall of Moses. As soon as we start deviating from the plan of God, we will miss it, and we will fall into disobedience. If we continue reading in the next verse, we will see Numbers 20:11 (KJV): "and Moses lifted up his hand, and with his rod he smote the rock twice: and the water came out abundantly, and the congregation, and their beasts drank."

You can see that Moses did eight things to God's five-step plan of instructions. *How many things, too many?* Of course that is three things too many. God never told Moses to raise his hand. God never told Moses to strike the rock. *Why did Moses have to hit the rock twice?* I think it was simply because nothing happened the first time Moses hit the rock. I believe that God realized that Moses was not going to follow the plan, so he was merciful and gave them water to drink anyway. Moses had to hit the rock twice before anything came out, and I bet you that Moses was a little concerned after nothing happened the first time that he struck the rock. What we must realize is that even though God still gave the people a drink, the actions taken by Moses had grave consequences attached to them. *What was God's response to Moses and Aaron's actions taken? Was God pleased?* Of course not. God says something that is very profound in Numbers 20:12 (KJV): "And the LORD spake unto Moses and Aaron, because ye believed me not, to sanctify me in the eyes of the children of Israel, therefore ye shall not bring this congregation into the land which I have given them."

God reveals the reason Moses struck the rock instead of speaking to the rock as being a case of his unbelief. Moses apparently had a problem with speaking to an inanimate object and expecting anything to happen from just your spoken words. I will bet you a lot of us are still like Moses today. God was trying to teach his servant Moses a valuable lesson about the spiritual law of words. Words have authority and power behind them, and God was attempting to raise Moses's expectation level and spiritual awareness. We know that previously in the wilderness that God had told Moses to strike the rock to bring out water for the people, but this time God changed the plan.

Following the instructions of God is very important to the successful outcome of any task we are given to do—if not the consequences, can be very devastating. Several years ago, I went on a trip to Ashland, Virginia's campgrounds with several people from my church. It was my first time visiting a spiritual retreat. My experiences there with God were greater than my imagination could ever capture. So when God gave me a specific instruction during prayer for two of the ladies who were sick from different elements, instead of doing what God instructed me to do, I proceeded to alter the instruction a little. The outcome was not good.

Here is what happened: A group of us met in one sister's room for prayer. We were praying for many things and people. Then the group put one of the ladies (we will call her Lady 1) who had some health problems in the center of the room, where we circled around her. I was not aware of this person's health problems until that moment, and I was not aware of the other woman (we will call her Lady 2) health problems until after the Lord gave me the instruction for her. By the way, Lady 2 was not part of the group of women praying in the room.

In the process of praying for Lady 1, the Lord began to give me an instruction for her. He said tell Lady 1 to pray for Lady 2, and he would heal her (Lady 1). That was the instruction given to me. Quite simple. *Right?* Like Moses, I started out following the instructions God gave me for the ladies, then I began to add my spin to it. I did told Lady 1 that God told me to tell her to pray for Lady 2 and that he would heal her. I do not know if she ever prayed for Lady 2. I do not think she believed me anyway.

Once the group prayer session was over, I went back to my room with some of the women who were sharing the room with me, and then I went to seek out Lady 2 to tell her what God said. When I told her what God had told me to do, she was truly angry. I was so shocked from her reaction I started to cry. I was not crying because she was upset; I was crying because I thought God had given me a simple instruction that I could not carry out. He never told me to speak to Lady 2, and it was obvious from her response that she did not want anyone to know about her health problems.

Did any of these women ever get healed? For Lady 1, her problem continues for many years, but today I believe God may have healed her. For Lady 2, I do not know, but his grace despite our disobedience is sufficient for the day. *So why did I add to the instruction?* Simple. Like Moses, I did not expect anything to happen from just my spoken words. I did not believe Lady 1 would believe that God spoke to me, so I took the instruction to Lady 2, and the outcome was unpleasant.

If you have not realized it, God hardly ever does the same things twice. By God's instructions, Moses was supposed to speak to the rock before the people. As my instruction was to speak to Lady 1, so while the people were watching, the people would have learned a valuable spiritual lesson also. But Moses failed, and as a result, God told him that he would not enter the Promised Land that he had already given to them. For those two women, my disobedience did not bring them the healing they could have otherwise had immediately. God reveals to Moses a spiritual law concerning the words that he speaks. This spiritual law applies across the board to everyone in the congregation as well as the leadership. God told Moses that he would do whatever Moses said.

This verse tells me that God listens to the words that come out of our mouths. Whatever you say, that is what God will do for you. It amazes me when I study the Bible like this and see God's response to what people say. I know there are other spiritual laws in the Bible also; this one is not the only spiritual law that affects what people get in life. But this one is certainly one of the ones that people do not have a clue about.

The Power of Spoken Word

One of the most important subjects in the Bible to study and to understand is about your spoken words. Spoken words have no physical forms but have the power to destroy. Our words travel through different spiritual dimensions, and like all seeds, once they take root, they will form for us or against us. God tells us that he is listening to what we say and that he will do to us whatever we say. If we speak evil, that is what we will get. If we speak good things, that is also what we will get. Our words only affect our outcome and what we get.

Because the children of Israel murmured and complained to God about their situation, that was what they got. The older generation did not enter the Promised Land, except for Joshua and Caleb. *What made Joshua and Caleb different? What caused Joshua and Caleb to enter in where the other people their age all died?* They were the two spies who brought back a good report and believed God would help them succeed. God did to Joshua and Caleb what they said, and the others also got what they said. This is a prevalent reality found throughout the Bible, from cover to cover. You can read practically any story in the Bible, and you can observe very closely exactly what they say then read ahead and see what they got in life.[4]

When we see patterns in our lives, it is necessary to find where (the location) the root of the problem lies, not what the problem is. If you look at what you have today and analyze it with what you said in the past, it will almost always add up to the same results. Even though our words are a gift, they do have the power to destroy and the power to build up (Prov. 12:6, NKJV). The writer of Proverbs tells us, "The tongue has the power of life and death, and those who love it will eat its fruit" (Prov. 18:21, NKJV). *Are we using words to build up people or destroy them? Are they filled with hate or love, bitterness or blessings? Complaining or compliments, lust or love, victory or defeat?* Like tools, they can be used to help us reach our goals or to send us spiraling into a deep depression.[4]

Words have more power than we customarily attribute to them. They go forth with a tremor that can be heartbreaking, comforting, healing, encouraging, or depressing, causing hostility, damaging, and discouraging. Whatever the level of tremor, it goes out into space and lingers there, affecting the atmosphere surrounding us. You have probably experienced this. Therefore, if we want to produce goodness in our world, it is important that the words we speak and the thoughts we engage reflect that quality. Of course our lives need to be in alignment with the qualities we are invoking. We cannot be decreeing to change and balance past negative atmosphere at the same time we are consciously creating more negative atmosphere and expect to be making any progress.

There needs to be a certain degree of striving to attain the qualities we are calling forth and, at the same time, the absolute conviction that the call does force the answer. Furthermore, our words have the power to bring us death or life not only in this world but in the next as well. Jesus said, "But I tell you that men will have to give account on the day of judgment for every careless word they have spoken. For by your words you will be acquitted, and by your words you will be condemned" (Matt. 12:36–37, NKJV). Words are so important that we are going to give an account of what we say when we stand before the Lord Jesus Christ. Jesus reminds us that the words we speak are actually the overflow of our hearts (Matt. 12:34–35, NKJV). As stated in 1 John 1:1–4 (NKJV), Jesus was the word, and the word became flesh and dwelled among us. The words we speak have the same power once they come out of our mouths. They travel through different dimensions and space until they find someone to connect with to manifest that word we speak and dwell among us.[4]

> *What was from the beginning, what we have heard, what we have seen with our eyes, what we have looked at and travels touched with our hands, concerning the Word of Life. and the life was manifested, and we have seen and testify and proclaim to you the eternal life, which was with the Father and was manifested to us. what we have seen and heard we proclaim to you also, so that you too may have fellowship with us…that our joy may be made complete* (1 John 1:1–4, NKJV).

Sometimes we speak negatively about ourselves or about someone, and before we know it, they show up in our lives and treat us the way we speak and think of ourselves. *Then we begin to wonder, "Why is this person treating me this way?" "What did I ever do to them?"* We are what happened. We spoke negatively against ourselves or circumstances, and those spoken words are now dwelling among us. We are the ones who invite them in our lives by the words we speak. We get exactly what we have been proclaiming, the Incarnate Word.

The reason the word became flesh and dwelled among us is that the spoken word cannot return void until it accomplishes what it is set out to do. It may take days, weeks, months, or years, but if we continue to put out those word seeds, negative or positive, they will eventually bear fruit in the form of a person who dwells among us to make those words our reality. God reveals it to Isaiah in chapter 55, verse 11 (NKJV): "So shall my words be that goeth forth out of my mouth; it shall not return onto me void, but it shall accomplish that which I please, and it shall prosper in the things whereto I sent it."

Many of you will say this only applies to God who is sovereign, and the word he spoke cannot return void until it accomplishes its task, and that is true. However, God himself gave us power and authority in the earth, so when we speak, it is like God speaking; every element in the earth must respond to what we put out there. Once I received this revelation, I understood the reasons I had so many obstacles, delays, and blockages in certain areas of my life. People, including myself, have spoken negative words against me that have formed spiritual weapons that have fought me all the way.

The more frustrated I became within my state of paralysis, situations, and circumstances that were not working out as I expected, the more negative my word would be against myself. Couple that with what other people who do not like me, and even those who claim they love me. Out of their ignorance, I have spoken against myself and contribute to me struggles. Ecclesiastes 5:2 (NKJV) says, "Be not rash with thy mouth and let not thine heart be hasty to utter anything before God: for God is in heaven, and thou upon earth: therefore, let thy words be few." This verse starts with do not be "rash" with your mouth! *Did you know that we can be rash with our mouths?* The swords of our mouths can cut two ways, either blessing someone or cursing someone. This is the power that we have in our mouths, according to the Bible.

We should always speak blessings over our children and encourage them with our words. There are many children in our world who have never heard their parents say they were proud of them. There are many children in the world who have never been told that they have great potential to do great things in the world. These are the children who have been cursed by their parents, saying they are stupid, dumb, and incapable of anything positive. These are examples of "rash" words being spoken in the world.

When one becomes a Christian, there is an expectation that a change of speech follows because living for Christ makes a difference in one's choice of words. The sinner's mouth is "full of cursing and bitterness" (Rom. 3:14, NKJV), but when we turn our lives over to Christ, we gladly confess that "Jesus is Lord" (Rom. 10:9–10, NKJV). As condemned sinners, our mouths are silenced before the throne of God (Rom. 3:19, NKJV), but as believers, our mouths are opened to praise and glorify God (Rom. 15:6, NKJV).[4]

The book of Ecclesiastes shows us how spoken words and their connection to our relationship with God and the need to align our words to our actions for the continued blessings of God to come upon and overtake us. What we say has more bearings on what we obtain out of life than anything else that we do here. I know it is not easy to always speak positive, uplifting word about ourselves consistently, but we must do that to change the negativity in our lives. We can start by appreciating the good things about ourselves. We all have many good qualities we can push forward and work on our weakness so they, too, can become our strength. Learn to be quick to hear from God and slow to speak so that you can continue to learn from him. Let your words be few in general to everyone. If you have nothing good to say to or about someone, it's best to say nothing.[5]

Make My Enemy a Footstool

According to Jesus in Luke 20:42–43 (NKJV), David himself declares in the book of Psalms, "The LORD said to my Lord: 'Sit at my right hand until I make your enemies a footstool for your feet.'" *What exactly does this statement means?* It was a common practice in biblical times that a conquering king would put his foot on the neck of his surviving enemy leaders, hence the term "footstool." The Son will put his foot on the neck of his enemies until the final enemy (death) is defeated. *Powerful statement! Do you think? So why are we not more successful in the defeating the enemies in our lives?*

I have heard many pastors teaching on this chapter, but none like Bishop Christian Winters, senior pastor at Master Builders Church in Philadelphia. I was invited by one of our participants from the Transform Your Mind Program to fellowship with them. One of the reasons our prison program is so successful is because I make it our businesses to get involved in the lives of the participants and their families. This builds trust among the family members and myself, so when the participant is not doing the "right thing," I can expect a call from a mother, a girlfriend, or a wife. This gesture is called accountability, and we all need to be accountable to someone or something.

I had never really given much thought to what a footstool does, and if you had asked me before my new knowledge, I would have said something to put my feet on. But according to Pastor Winters, a footstool is something we use to reach for something. So if I am going to achieve any success in my life or to see the manifestations of what I believe God has for me, there are certain things I must do. First, I cannot become what I want to be until I make my enemy my footstool. *So what must I do to make my enemy my footstool?* Know my enemy; the enemy is that person, habit, or thing I cannot walk away from or say no to.

According to dictionary.com, an enemy is a "person who feels hatred for, fosters harmful designs against, or engages in antagonistic activities against another; an adversary or opponent." The enemy inside us or outside us is something we normally try to avoid. However, there is a greater high in life, and for us to get there, we must reach higher. We must confront the things that bring embarrassment and shame upon us. The thing that makes us say if I did not do that, I would be a better person. The things the enemy keeps rewinding in our minds, which bring condemnation and paralyze us from moving to a higher state of mind and a higher practice of personal character.

Everything in our lives requires us to go higher. God will continually say to us to come up higher. In Revelation 4:1 (NKJV), God said, "Come up here, and I will show you things which must take place." Oswald Chambers explained it eloquently when he said God was not the only one calling us to go higher, that there is also a continuing rule in temptation that calls us to go higher. However, when we do, we only encounter other temptations and character traits. Both God and the enemy use the strategy of elevation, but Satan uses it in temptation, and the effect is quite different. If we yield to the devil temptations, it will elevate us to a certain place that causes us to fasten our idea of what holiness is far beyond what flesh and blood could ever bear or achieve. Our lives become a spiritual acrobatic performance high atop a steeple. We cling to it, trying to maintain our balance and daring not to move. But when God elevates us by his grace into heavenly places, we find a vast plateau where we can move about with ease.

How do I act on this level so that what I want to become is reachable? Believe God, and do not give up. Keep fighting until you concur your fears, addictions, or whatever it is that is keeping you from moving to the next level in your life. It is important for you to understand that just walking away from a problem, crisis, or weakness without dealing with issue is not a victory; in fact, it is a defeat because at the end of the day, you have not changed. We need to stop seeing our problems as giants and walk in the revelation that whatever we need God to do for us has already been done because Jesus has accomplished all for us. The vision given to me by God requires that I elevate to a higher state of mind and character so when temptations comes before me, I need to immediately give it to God. He is the only one who can shine his light in the dark places of my life and your life that is preventing us from making our enemy our footstool and elevates us to a higher level. And God is asking, "In spite of the giants, would you go up and enter the promised land of my rest? We must learn to be rest conscious rather than giant conscious." God does not say, "Wait until all your enemies have been destroyed until every problem in your life has been resolved, then you can rest." He says, "Rest first until I make all your enemies your footstool."

Seek rest first that it may be well. Now if we do not cease from our works, we have not entered into his rest. He who has entered into it has ceased from work, even as God ceased from his own works when he entered into his rest. We find it hard to rest because our human nature is inclined toward worry and restlessness. The devil loves to see human nature reign in the church and to have us believe that we can only rest when things go well or when we see your breakthrough. Believers in Christ *enter rest* and have the hope of the promised rest. To have the rest is conditioned upon a trusting faith.

Therefore, since a promise remains of entering his rest, let us fear lest any of us seem to have come short of it. For indeed the gospel was preached to us as well as to them, but the word, which they heard, did not profit them, not being mixed with faith in those who heard it. The idea is carried on without pause from Hebrews 3, that unbelief kept the generation that escaped Egypt from entering Canaan. *The promise remains of entering his rest,* and we can enter into that *rest* by faith. Unbelief will make us fall short of the *rest* God has for us.

Yielding

Right living first comes from what I believe of myself, and what I believe of myself comes from what I have been told about myself. The first thing I had to do was admit about things that have control over me and dominate me and that I am the one responsible for having yielded myself to whatever they might be. Somewhere in my past, I yielded to myself. Likewise, if I obey God, I do so because at some point in my life, I yielded myself to him.[2] During my state of paralysis, I forgot what God said about me and who I am to him, and the enemy naturally has no problem building up the lies based on the condition of my heart. So I yielded to the nature of the lust in my life, and although I may hate myself for having yielded, I became enslaved to that lust. Lust is "I must have it now," whether it is the lust of the flesh or the lust of the mind. Once we yield to something, we will soon realize the tremendous control it has over us. Even though we believe we can give up that habit whenever we like, we eventually know we cannot. The habit dominates us because we willingly yielded. Before we can enter God rest, we first must yield to him, and we can only do that through faith.[5]

God tells me to spend my time thinking about what he said about me and not the lies of my enemy. By yielding to Jesus, he will break every kind of slavery in my life. No release or escape from it will ever come from any human power but only through the power of redemption. I must yield myself in utter humiliation to the only one who can break the dominating power in my life, namely, the Lord Jesus Christ. Luke 4:18 and Isaiah 61:1 (NKJV) states, "He has anointed Me to proclaim liberty to the captives." Meditate on these scriptures and keep them in your heart.

I want to share Psalm 119:114 (NKJV): "You are my refuge and my shield. I have put my hope in your Word."[5] As someone whom God had to literally force to surrender to him, this is a very painful and heartbreaking process, but now after going through it, I realized it was a necessary for him to do what he had to do. Otherwise, I would still be in state of paralysis, unable to fulfill the purpose and destiny of which he has called me. *Have you been propping up that foolish soul of yours with the idea that your circumstances are too much for God to handle?* Set all your opinions and speculations aside and "abide under the shadow of the Almighty" (Ps. 91:1, NKJV). Tell God you will not worry or fret about whatever concerns you anymore. Besides, planning without God causes all our worrying.

How do I accomplish this, Lord? I have lost my confidence, my faith, and my belief in you in my state of paralysis and confusion. *How do I break the stronghold of my mind?*

Jesus answered, "Just trust me again to lead you, and I will take you there. Trust me to turn your wilderness into standing water and your dry ground into water springs. The promise that I gave Joshua that day he led the Israelites out of the wilderness to the promise land is no less true for you now. Just like Moses and Joshua, I will be with you. I will not give up on you; I will not leave you. With strength! And courage! You are going to accomplish the vision I called you to do. Give it everything you have, heart and soul. Make sure you carry out the revelation that I gave you, every bit of it. Do not get off track, either left or right. Make sure you get to where you are going. And do not for a minute let this book of Revelation be out of mind. Ponder and meditate on it day and night, making sure you practice everything written in it. Then you will get where you are going; then you will succeed. Haven't I commanded you? Strength! Courage! Do not be fearful; do not get discouraged. God, your God, is with you every step you take."

I thought, O Lord, as I try to remember where in the Bible a scripture says, "Before I was afflicted, I went astray, but now have I kept thy word" (Ps. 119:67, KJV). I called upon the Lord in my distress, and the Lord answered me. The Lord who kept me, he will not slumber or sleep. He shall preserve my soul. I wept because I realized I have been paralyzed for so long and was not aware of it until now. In Colossians 2:6 (NKJV), we have God's confirmed answer: "As you have therefore received Christ Jesus the Lord, so walk you in him."

I walk in Jesus the same way I receive him, by simple faith. I simply took Jesus at his word and trust him to save me. I must see all my help in God; from him I must expect it, in his own way and time. *Did he say he is my God?* Not just God but my God. Suddenly it has a different meaning for me, the word my God indicates ownership. He is mine and I am his—we are one. What belongs to him also belongs to me. Scriptures teach us to comfort ourselves in the Lord when difficulties and dangers are greatest. It is almighty wisdom that contrives and almighty power that works the safety of those who put themselves under his protection. God is a wakeful, watchful keeper; he is never weary. Under his shade, we may sit with delight and assurance. He is always near us for our protection and refreshment. He will take care that we his children shall not fall.

With my confidence and hope once again in God, I know now that instead of being a mistake, I am the Lord's treasured possession. I memorize scripture and fill my mind with the truth of who God says I am. This understanding has made all the difference in my life. Now I recognize that God has a plan for my life, and he created me just the way I am for his special purpose. Scripture such as Jeremiah 31:3 (NKJV) says the Lord appeared to him from far away; I have loved you with an everlasting love; therefore, I have continued my faithfulness to you. Isaiah 43:4–5 (NKJV) says you are precious in my eyes, and honored, and I love you. I give men in return for you, peoples in exchange for your life. Fear not, for I am with you; I will bring your offspring from the east and from the west. I will gather you. And Romans 8:28 (NKJV) says we know that for those who love God, all things work together for good, for those who are called according to his purpose.

With my confidence once again in God, I can now take up my bed and walk to the place of victory, fulfillment, and satisfaction. The prayer below was developed while I was writing this chapter, having come to a greater understanding of the many barriers that have had a stronghold on my mind and of the freedom and power that is now unleashed in my life to reverse what was stifling me. The prayer is a wonderful reminder of where my help cometh. Oh, liberating to finally be free…

Breakthrough Prayer
(Pray it out loud every day)

Dear Heavenly Father,

I come before you to ask for forgiveness for not praying your will for my life.

I pray for the spirit of wisdom and revelation that I may know you better.

I pray also that the eyes of my heart may be enlightened in order that I may know the hope to which you have called me, the riches of your glorious inheritance in the saints and your incomparably great power for us who believe.

I also repent and ask for forgiveness for my ancestors and for this present generation that have violated our covenant with you and did not sow our seed in your Kingdom that has changed the atmosphere in our family line and created a climate of:

poverty, sickness, diseases, children out of marriage, separation, divorce, sexual immorality, lack of homes and businesses, premature death, debts, and depression.

Forgive us, O Lord, and break these climates in the sacrificial blood of Jesus Christ.

Amen.

(Negative Word Seed)

I also come against and take authority of all negative demonic word seed and powers

that have taken or blocked the financial flow in my life, the life of my children, and

my businesses. I cancel out all the negative word seed that has formed against me, my

family, and my businesses, in all the dimensions in the earth, under the earth, above

the earth and principalities. It is written in Isaiah 54:17, "No weapon formed against

me shall prosper; and every tongue that shall rise against me in judgment Thou shall

condemn. This is the heritage of the servants of the LORD and my vindication is from

Him, declares the LORD." In the name of Jesus,

Amen.

(Positive Word Seed)
to replace the negative

I conceive, give birth, and release the new word seed in all the dimensions in the earth,

under the earth, and above the earth and principalities by the power of Jesus Christ:

I am blessed coming in, and I am blessed going out. I am the head and not the tail.

No sickness or diseases shall befall me. I am the lender and not the borrower.

I have all power and authority through Jesus Christ in all the dimensions of the

earth and principalities. I shall decree and declare a thing, and it shall come to pass.

Everything my hands touch shall prosper; I have no lack in my life.

My family is blessed and highly favored.

My business is blessed.

My bank accounts are plenteous.

I command the wealth of the wicked to flow to me now.

I am a money magnet; money cometh to me.

Today I expect a miracle in my life

in the mighty name of Jesus.

Amen.

ENDNOTES

1   Paralysis facts and figures, Spinal Cord and Brain Injury Research, *Christopher and Dana Reeve Foundation*, christopherreeve.org, accessed February 24, 2014.

2   Henry George Liddell and Robert Scott, "παράλυσις," A Greek-English Lexicon (Oxford Clarendon Press on Perseus, 1940).

3   National Earth Science Teachers Association, https.

4   http://www.gotquestions.org/power-of-words.html#ixzz2vakvDMVD

5   Oswald Chambers, "Total Surrender," *My Utmost for His Highest* (Oswald Chambers Publications, 1992).

CHAPTER SIXTEEN

THE MANIFESTATIONS

The journey to my destiny is never easy, and it is rarely ever simple. It is truly a fight, but if I am going to be all that I was created for and to be a witness to the manifestation of the promise in my life, I had to take risks. The risks of being vulnerable about my weaknesses, uncertain about myself, but willing to push my way forward even in the presence of fear and pain. The journey did become more crystallized once I realized that all things and events hold intrinsic purpose, and for even one of them to go missing, this would tear a huge gulf into the very fabric of time and space.

God sent each of us to this planet carrying a portion of the creator's light inside. Only right now, that light is covered up by the flesh suit we call the human body. The question is, will we be able to look past the body and then be able to discern, develop, and nurture the light we each carry? It is not easy, I know! But learning how to succeed in this quest is part of God's plan and how we are helped to mature in the Spirit. I, for example, was sent to earth to expand, to be great, and to fulfill my destiny so God can be glorified. That destiny is to have a greater capacity for love so I can give it back to the word and change the lives of those who come into my space.

Sounds like a large order, and it is. That is why I believe God gives us vision, even though there are times during the process of fulfilling my destiny when it might look like it is all a lie. At those times, when it appears that God must have forgotten about me or that I must have misunderstood him and there is no way the vision is coming to pass, I refused to give up, I refused to let go from the vision he showed me, I refused to release myself from the light.

It took me a long time to learn this, but on my journey, I also discover what an amazing being in creation I am. There is no one like me in God's super universe, and there will never be again. I am so important to all of God's plans that if I were not here on earth, God could not complete his purpose in the earth. I know…incredible, right? Well, it is true, and the most wonderful thing about it, God would have it no other way! I am loved that much! And so are you! I undeniably understood that each one of us exists for a very definite purpose and holds a kind of unique energy that usually manifests as a kind of talent that is meant to be used and shared with others. It became clear to me that we are not just given the gift of physical life so that we can obtain a singular, self-focused experience but so that we might also use, share, and bequeath our own individuality, talents, and life to help others "experience life" for themselves.

The manifestation of the promise I found out does not come in one big package; it unfolds slowly in layer mostly because I respond slowly to God's instructions, and there are times when I am not so sure. So I am learning in the process of writing this book to believe God and everything he said, and no matter what it looks like, I need to remain confident in God's promise: "I AM GOING TO BLESS YOU."

I am also learning that if I do not trust God in the process, then I do not deserve the promise, and there is a difference between making something happen and letting something happen. God promises he would bless me, but I cannot have the promise without the process. By the way, that was the purpose God had in mind for me when he placed this book in my spirit to write. That purpose is to learn more about him and to learn more about myself and what it would require of me to fulfill my destiny. The question about our destiny is made more complex by our own lack of understanding about the nature of the supernatural that controls our lives. We tend to place our trust in explanations that provide the most appealing answer. Unfortunately, the truth about our future destiny is not always so apparent.

The vision that God gave me that will eventually lead me to my destiny is a progressive one because God gives it to me in parts. As I understand it, he released more to me. In Matthew 4:19 (NIV), Jesus said, "Come, follow me and I will send you out to fish for people." What Jesus was saying here to the disciples is this: "Follow me, and in the process, I will teach you how to be fishers of men." Many of us only hear the words "follow Me" but ignore the process of becoming fishers of men.[1]

A vision from God is always redemptive in nature, it involves others, and it involves restoring others' lives. A vision from God also shows us that we are all counted because the vision requires us helping others. *How do I accomplish this vision given to me by God?* The first thing I need to do is to see how Jesus accomplished his destiny on earth while he was here and to ask "How can I develop my mind to think and see life like Christ sees it?" In other words, my mind must exist in the highest spiritual mind of consciousness of love, which always seeks to create miracles for the higher self and for others at the same exact time.[2]

This higher spiritual mind of consciousness is not interested in personal benefits or ambitious indulgences of any kind. It does not feel it has to be. This type of thinkers deeply knows there is no greater act than the one that seeks to bestow the energy of great generosity. Grace, kindness, and love in the world, as sustaining this way of being, always create an energy of abundance for all in the end. Once you have become a person who has experienced and embraced your own holiness, only the vast, open sky is the limit as far as all the things you will be able to achieve and accomplish in a single lifetime. The rates to which we learn these principles is directly proportional to the rate at which we surrender. As Jesus said in the garden of Gethsemane, "Not My Will, but Yours, be done." As the ultimate example, Jesus leads the way in showing us the struggle between the flesh and the spirit. Therefore, when in doubt, we should always deny the flesh and say yes to the spirit. When we get to this level of spiritual maturity, the seed of the faith now produces the fruit.[2]

This is what was meant by the prophecy I received: "As my soul becomes like a watered garden and the soil of my life yields immediately the fruit of the seed that was sown into it, it's demonstration time! It is manifestation time! It's the experience time of victory 100 percent of the time." I will explain the prophecy later in this chapter.

Those of us who can sustain this form of consciousness in life are the miracle workers of the world, and in the process of being alive, many, many lives are healed, transformed, restored, and greatly blessed because of us. Wherever we go, we fill the atmosphere with the energy of hope. Once recognized, it is easy to see why the concept of higher-spiritual-minded people is such a hugely beneficial stream of consciousness, because of its lures toward us and others of similar vibration and frequency, and together we can do great things. Many of us who work from a higher spiritual mind of consciousness will always be spiritually led and, because of this, are able to seek and follow a more pure and divine path, which perpetually leads to the right actions when solving problems.[2]

I notice as older and more experienced and mature my own soul becomes, it is learning how to balance all the arrears of my life; as a result, the more increase my revelation experiences. This is such a normal part of my life now that I will feel as if something is missing if I am without a revelatory experience for too long. And if I am, this simply means I need balancing, or I need to amend something in my life that might be blocking me.

Through each of us living in a physical body and having been given a unique personality, we are not only helped to better understand our creator, but this is how we are encouraged to learn how to recognize and start practicing love. As we struggle yet seek to take dominion over the ego, we learn to recognize the voice of our own spirit while learning how to differentiate between the needs versus the wants of our own soul. (And yes, there is a difference as our "wants" tend to be more ego-motivated.) If love is truly utilized and practiced as we seek to manifest our needs in a balanced way, we will then begin a more lasting and resourceful relationship with our own spirit, which over time will help us expand our consciousness and self-awareness, thus helping each of us to better understand our life's true purpose.[2]

The Process to the Manifestation

During this process, the Holy Spirit of God would direct me to different scriptures for encouragement and understanding of where God was intending to take me. When God gives me a word, there are three ways for me to interpret that message, which help me determine whether that word is for that time (dispensational), whether I should take that word literally (as it is, for example, in the commandment, "Thou shalt not kill") or is it spiritual (like taking communion). Whichever interpretation I use, I need to understand that God's message is always for me, and as I surrender to God truth, that message will be universalities into my ministry for the world. The message from God always becomes more universal, but first it must come to me, and I must accept it.

For example, six years ago, when I was writing my first book on Philadelphia, God gave me the scripture from Revelation 3:7–13 (NKJV). I was not as mature in the word as I am today, so I took it literally for Philadelphia, and it is. However, before the message can become universal, it is for me first, and as I surrender to God truth, that message will be universalities into my ministry for the world, starting with Philadelphia.

The Faithful Church

Revelation 3:7–13 (NKJV) states,

And to the angel of the church in Philadelphia write, 'These things says He who is holy, He who is true, He who has the key of David, He who opens and no one shuts, and shuts and no one opens": I know your works. See, I have set before you an open door, and no one can shut it; for you have a little strength, have kept My word, and have not denied My name. Indeed I will make those of the synagogue of Satan, who say they are Jews and are not, but lie—indeed I will make them come and worship before your feet, and to know that I have loved you. Because you have kept My command to persevere, I also will keep you from the hour of trial which shall come upon the whole world, to test those who dwell on the earth. Behold, I am coming quickly! Hold fast what you have, that no one may take your crown. He who overcomes, I will make him a pillar in the temple of My God, and he shall go out no more. I will write on him the name of My God and the name of the city of My God, the New Jerusalem, which comes down out of heaven from My God. And I will write on him My new name. "He who has an ear, let him hear what the Spirit says to the churches."

Here I am eight years later, writing my second book and experiencing tremendous challenges. Along the way, the Holy Spirit would take me to different scriptures to encourage me to stay the course. One day I was in the book of 2 Kings when I came across the story of Hezekiah in 20:1–12 (NKJV). I thought if God can change his mind and make this man live after he was scheduled for death, surely I could make my case to God too. I was not sick, and I do not have any deadly illnesses, but I felt God was no longer listening to me, and I thought my prayers were not being answered. I noticed in verse 3 that Hezekiah was making his case to God: "Remember, LORD, how I have walked before you faithfully and with wholehearted devotion and have done what is good in your eyes." And Hezekiah wept bitterly. I thought, God, I have not always done what is good in your eyes. I cannot use this to make my case. I went to bed thinking about this. In the next morning, as I fellowshipped with the Lord, the Holy Spirit directed me to Psalm 40:9–17 (NKJV), telling me, "This is your petition, you pray to the Lord. This is for you."

Psalm 40:9–17 (ESV)

I have told the glad news of deliverance in the great congregation; behold, I have not restrained my lips, as you know, O Lord. I have not hidden your deliverance within my heart; I have spoken of your faithfulness and your salvation; I have not concealed your steadfast love and your faithfulness from the great congregation. As for you, O Lord, you will not restrain your mercy from me; your steadfast love and your faithfulness will ever preserve me! For evils have encompassed me beyond number; my iniquities have overtaken me, and I cannot see; they are more than the hairs of my head; my heart fails me. Be pleased, O Lord, to deliver me! O Lord make haste to help me! Let those be put to shame and disappointed altogether who seek to snatch away my life; let those be turned back and brought to dishonor who delight in my hurt! Let those be appalled because of their shame who say to me, "Aha, Aha!" But may all who seek you rejoice and be glad in you; may those who love your salvation say continually, "Great is the Lord!" As for me, I am poor and needy, but the Lord takes thought for me. You are my help and my deliverer; do not delay, O my God!

Each day after, this verse became my petition to God. How amazing God is. I am surely not perfect, but I have done many things that please him. Enough for me to make my case before God, and he himself is revealing it to me. Understand that Jesus Christ already paid the price for my sins that is not what I am talking about; however, I still must give God account for the things I do here on earth. About two years ago, my bishop, C. Milton Grannum, taught on Isaiah 58 (NKJV) the fast God requires. Recently the Lord kept bringing it to my remembrance, so I decided to take the time to study Isaiah 58:1–14 (NKJV). I especially focused on verses 6–14, the fast the Lord said he requires.

Is this not the fast that I have chosen: To lose the bonds of wickedness, to undo the heavy burdens, To let the oppressed go free, And that you break every yoke? Is it not to share your bread with the hungry, And that you bring to your house the poor who are cast out; When you see the naked, that you cover him, And not hide yourself from your own flesh? Then your light shall break forth like the morning, Your healing shall spring forth speedily, and your righteousness shall go before you; The glory of the LORD shall be your rear guard. Then you shall call, and the LORD will answer; You shall cry, and He will say, "Here I am." "If you take away the yoke from your midst, The pointing of the finger, and speaking wickedness,

If you extend your soul to the hungry And satisfy the afflicted soul, Then your light shall dawn in the darkness, And your darkness shall be as the noonday. The LORD will guide you continually, and satisfy your soul in drought, And strengthen your bones; You shall be like a watered garden, And like a spring of water, whose waters do not fail.

Those from among you Shall build the old waste places; You shall raise up the foundations of many generations; And you shall be called the Repairer of the Breach, The Restorer of Streets to Dwell In. "If you turn away your foot from the Sabbath, From doing your pleasure on My holy day, And call the Sabbath a delight, The holy day of the LORD honorable, And shall honor Him, not doing your own ways, Nor finding your own pleasure, Nor speaking your own words, Then you shall delight yourself in the LORD; And I will cause you to ride on the high hills of the earth, And feed you with the heritage of Jacob your father. The mouth of the LORD has spoken."

This is what I do daily, I thought to myself. The fast God requires is what I do. This is my life work, so why am not walking into the blessing from doing such a fast? It took me months of reading and mediating on this scripture for me to see that this scripture was about my "breakthrough"—what I had to do, what he called me to do, and how God would respond to me after I fulfill his desires. The big question for me is, how do I get the blessing of Isaiah 58 to manifest in my life? A whole lot of grace and a whole lot of faith no doubt. But do I know how to pull on grace and activate my faith to pull these blessings into my reality?

I found out I was wrong about so many things; what a journey this has been for me. My confidence and trust in God is stronger than it has ever been, yet at times fear tries to come into my heart. It is amazing how the mind works. I constantly must remind myself who I am versus what the mind wants to tell me who I am. How true the statement Pastor Joel Osteen made in his sermon one Sunday. He said whatever follows "I am" will find you. I am now learning to change the "I am" that comes out of my mouth so I do not sabotage my own destiny.

God did not say the manifestations of his promises would be released immediately because I believe. But I can be confident in knowing that if I ask God for something, God *always* hears me and wants to make me happy; therefore at some point (whether it is in this lifetime or another), my desires will be granted.

The challenge now is for me to stand like Habakkuk did. "I will stand at my watch post, and station myself on the rampart; I will keep watch to see what He will say to me, and what he will answer concerning my complaint." After all, God did warn me in Isaiah 55:8–11:

"For my thoughts are not your thoughts, neither are your ways my ways," declares the LORD. "As the heavens are higher than the earth, so are my ways higher than your ways and my thoughts than your thoughts. As the rain and the snow come down from heaven, and do not return to it without watering the earth and making it bud and flourish, so that it yields seed for the sower and bread for the eater, so is my word that goes out from my mouth: It will not return to me empty, but will accomplish what I desire and achieve the purpose for which I sent it.

That is so true, though in some things, there may be a likeness between the thoughts of God and the thoughts of men as to the nature of them. Thoughts are natural and essential to us as man; they are within us, are internal acts, and are unknown to others, still made known. But then the thoughts of men are finite and limited, whereas the thoughts of the Lord are infinite and boundless. Men's thoughts have a beginning, but the Lord's have none. No wonder the Lord commanded me to have strength and courage and not to be fearful or to get discouraged if I am going to fulfill my destiny.

I mentioned in the previous chapter that I would put this book aside and wait to see the manifestation of God's promises before I continue the final chapter. That is what I thought I should do until the Lord revealed to me that the manifestation that shows up in my life will base not only on what I believe but also on what I do. There are actions I must take before I will see the changes I seek in my life and the success of my ministries. My assurance during this process is knowing that the vision and the words God spoke over my life cannot return to him void. It will travel through dimensions, space, and principalities until it accomplishes its purpose in my life.

So what must I do to see the manifestation of what I believe in? First, I had to recognize that the manifestation already began. The minute I begun to write this book is when the manifestation began for me. God was unpeeling the layers of my life that was blocking my perception of him, forcing me to be bold by elevating my strength and confronting my weakness that was keeping me stumbling. Second, I had to receive the gifts God has given to me. There are many gifts that God has given to me that I had never accepted, certainly not with confidence.

The gift of prophecy is one of the gifts God has blessed me with, yet I refused to call myself a prophet until God himself said I was. He gave me the inspiration in 2009 to write a prophetic book about *Philadelphia, Release the Prophetic Destiny in Philadelphia: A City Under Reconstruction*, but until he told me I was called to be a prophet, I would tell people that God gave me the instructions, and I wrote them down. He never told me I was a prophet, so I refused to call myself one.

I have seen so many people in the church give themselves titles so they can feel good about themselves, to feel relevant and important. Many have left churches because they feel their gifts are not being exercised by the pastors. The truth is, we are all called to prophesy, and just in case any Christian is in doubt at all whether they can prophesy, the scripture makes it very clear: "For you can (or "may") all prophesy one by one, that all may learn, and all may be encouraged" (1 Cor. 14:31, NKJV).

I am a low-key person; the less attention that is on me, the better I like it. I do not mind doing the work, and I will always do it with excellence. I just do not want the spotlight on me. Finally, after waiting for the past five years for God to say to me, "I have called you as a prophetic," he did the first week of April 2014. He directed me to Jeremiah 1:5, 6–10:

> Before I formed thee in the belly, I knew thee, and before thou camest forth out of the womb I sanctified thee; I have appointed thee a prophet unto the nations. Be not afraid of them; for I am with thee to deliver thee, saith the LORD. Then the LORD put forth His hand, and touched my mouth; and the LORD said unto me: Behold, I have put My words in thy mouth; See, I have this day set thee over the nations and over the kingdoms, to root out and to pull down, and to destroy and to overthrow; to build, and to plant.

Wow! Now that he has said it, I can now receive it, this gift without repentance. I became inspired as I reflected on what this verse said about the omniscience of God. God is telling me that he "knew" me before I was formed within the womb. He already knew my strengths and weaknesses; he already knew that I possessed what he wanted to use during this particularly trying time in history. And before I was born, God had already set me aside for a special task, which he would give to me years later as an adult.

"The prophetic voice of God is revealed through the Gift of Prophecy functioning. The gift is for the edification ("oikodome" "to build up, the promotion of spiritual growth"), exhortation ("paraklesis" "encouragement, a calling near or for, to stir up") and comfort ("paramuthia" "a consolation, a solace ministered with tenderness"; "consolation" is "to alleviate grief or disappointment" and "solace" is "comfort in distress or disappointment, to find relief, cheer up") of the church. The prophetic voice is to be uttered with a simple yet clear understanding ~ clear and simple enough for the people to grasp what you are saying clearly. It is vital that we "catch" the prophetic words that come forth through the gift of Prophecy. We neglect it to our own hurt and hindrance in the things of God."[3]

The book I wrote about Philadelphia to date is not a best seller despite the many book signings, traveling around the country, and promotions we did, and now I know why. Even though I was obedience to God and wrote the book as it was instructed to me, I never accepted the gift of prophecy that God gave me until now. Until I came into agreement with God and accepted this gift that he gave me, this important book would remain an ordinary book. But

God's words must come forth, so on many occasions, we have prophets visited my church and prophesy about Philadelphia, and I would wonder, did they read my book?

Word for word they would repeat the very messages the Lord gave me for Philadelphia. Spiritual gifts are not innate, natural talents, like an ear for music or the ability to draw, but rather they are empowerments that the Holy Spirit gives to a believer to minister to the body in ways that were not possible by mere natural effort apart from the Holy Spirit. Therefore, my capacity and capability in spiritual matters is measured by and based on the promises of God. So even those people who have never read my book, God still provided the messages to them through the Holy Spirit.

All the gifts are needed in the body of Christ. All the gifts are equally valid. In 1 Corinthians 12:12 (NKJV), the apostle Paul instructs the church that no one should despise his/her own gift by comparing it with the gifts of others. And he also says that no one should despise someone else's gift as being less than his/her gift. Some gifts are more apparent than others, but each gift is important. In the ministry of the apostles in the book of Acts, we see that they performed miracles, healed people, preached, and spoke in tongues, which they had not been able to do apart from Christ.

If I get less than God wants me to have, I will falsely accuse him as the servant falsely accused his master when he said, "You expect more of me than you give me the power to do." I was allowing the limitations of my own natural abilities to enter my decision to receive the gift God gave me. Not realizing if I received the Holy Spirit, God expects the work of the Holy Spirit to be exhibited in me. By the way, now that I have accepted this gift from God; I have no doubt that *Release the Prophetic Destiny in Philadelphia* will be on the *New York Times* best seller's list very soon.

One day while I was researching on the supernatural, I came across a prophetic word from someone I have never met, Dr. Christian Harfouche. The moment I read it, I know it was for me, came straight from the book of Isaiah 58:6–11 (NKJV). I would like to share it with you. Dr. Harfouche said she received this prophetic word from God during her twenty days of forty days fast and prayer. She calls it seven certain, miraculous, divine breakthroughs. Oh yes!

MY SEVEN SUPERNATURAL BREAKTHROUGHS

Breakthrough #1: *As found in Isaiah 58:6–11, the Spirit of the Lord declares that there will be a breakthrough of health that will spring forth in your life.*

Breakthrough #2: *There will be a supernatural experience of God's protection. Not only will your spirit, soul, and body be healthy and flourishing, but your divine protection and the protection of your family, and your entire jurisdiction are guaranteed by God's holy Word.*

Breakthrough #3: There will be a breakthrough of answers from the Lord. Their speed and the rapidity with which they will take place will be unusual, and it will be supernaturally swift and immediate.

Breakthrough #4: God will give you promotion power. It will be power that will elevate your call, your standard of living, and your thirst and fire for God. There will be a promotion power in your life that cannot be short-circuited.

Breakthrough #5: This is the power of God's spiritual leadings. When we are directed by God, we are directed into triumph. We are directed into victory and we are directed into it all the time.

Breakthrough #6: The Lord told me to tell you that there will be a glorious supernatural satisfaction and refreshing in your life. You are coming into youth and zeal and revival; this is a renewal and vivification in your life. You are also coming into a place of satisfaction where you will say, "It is enough Lord." You will feel like it is too much, like it is too good! This is the promise of God's Word to you and it cannot be refuted. If God said it, we believe it and that settles it!

Breakthrough #7: The Lord is directing me to pronounce over you the overflowing, never ending, producing anointing of God over your life, that is right, your never-ending overflow. It is a productivity that comes from God, as your soul becomes like a watered garden and the soil of your life yields immediately the fruit of the seed that was sown into it. It is demonstration time! It is manifestation time! It is the experience time of Victory 100% of the time—never stopping short of your miracle!

Every morning during my worship, I would speak out these breakthroughs and receive these covenant blessings from God. One night as I lay in bed, my thought went to breakthrough #7, where it said, "As your soul becomes like a watered garden and the soil of your life yields immediately the fruit of the seed that was sown into it. It is demonstration time! It is manifestation time! It's the experience time of Victory 100% of the time." *What is God saying?* Before the manifestation or harvest, something must happen. "When the soil of my life yields immediately, the fruit of the seed that was sown into it, then the manifestation of all that I have believing God for will come forth."

So let us examine further. As your soul becomes like a watered garden, a watered garden represents something that is well attended to, beautiful, flourishing, and healthy. The seed that is sown in the soil of my life represent the Word of God, and when I yield to God in obedience and trust in his grace through faith, then it is demonstration time.

Even though I have done the fast God desires, interims of the work I do, I have not yet yielded all the arrears of my life to him. I must come to that place where I believe that God can take care of everything that concerns me. More importantly, I had to elevate my mind from thinking that my faith is something to get God to do something for me. The truth is, God does not need to be moved; everything I need is already done. Jesus Christ already on the cross makes the exchange; he took on my mess and gives me his goodness. My needs are already supplied before the need even exits, but it does not automatically show up.

I mentioned early in the chapter on faith that when it comes to healing, I have great faith in God to heal me or anyone I prayed for, and naturally I have faith in my salvation. God, however, requires that I have faith in him in all things. Without this kind of faith, I cannot please him. Faith is our response to what God already supply.

Faith only propagates what God already provided by grace. God provide grace through Jesus Christ. In Mark 11:23–24 (NKJV), Jesus said, "Truly I say to you, whoever says to this mountain, 'Be taken up and cast into the sea,' and does not doubt in his heart, but believes that what he says is going to happen, it will be granted to him. Therefore, I tell you, whatever you ask in prayer, believe that you have received it, and it will be yours."

So if God already provides what I need, it should take the struggle out of my faith. Therefore, I need to inquire from God where it is, and how do I get it, and the wisdom to know when it shows up. I am learning to take what is mine by grace through faith. We each have lots to do in this life, working with different people and developing various talents, and the result may be that we will not have enough time to accomplish every new goal or dream before this lifetime is completed. Therefore, we should keep in mind that God always knows when the best or exact time to have us receive a request would be. Our ego makes us believe that we should have what we want in the instant we made the request (especially during times when it seems we are suffering), but God always knows when "that something we want" would be more meaningful and have a more lasting impact, and these are the times when God usually gives us the desires of our heart. We must keep in mind that life is a whole lot bigger than our ego mind lets us think it is. Everything we endure in life is all about expanding our capacity, making us ready to be able to accommodate, even more once a request we made to God arrives.

Here is the amazing thing. For the longest time, I was afraid to totally let go and let God have control over my life. Here is what I am learning; when I yield my life to God, I am now opened to receive all that the universe has for me. Everything that belongs to God also belongs to me; therefore, everything in creation is waiting on me to respond to my requests. The angels are waiting to service me; the universe is waiting on release to me that which has been stored up for me.

The bottom line is this: we are his children, and God loves us unconditionally and will spare no expense to show us. Our part? Believe him! When we become inspired by the higher spiritual mind of consciousness, we do great things in both the earth realm and for the higher astral. As they occur, the light and love of God Almighty follow us wherever we go. We will be granted with tremendous wealth of wisdom, self-confidence in faith in both God and people. We will have doors of opportunity open for us that would seem impossible or beyond the reach for others. The perception we will have of our own lives and journey here will not be judged by using the world perception but of one that is divine, and we will find ourselves attaining the vision that yields a kind of happiness that is not of this world. So when we ask heaven to help us manifest a major dream, we must realize that the ones looking after them know that if the dream came when we were not truly ready for it, it would crush us! Therefore, heaven sends lessons and challenges to help us develop character and integrity.

Decree a Thing, and It Should Be Established

The word "decree" means to issue an edict to order or determine what is to be done in a particular matter. As I begin to mature in the Lord, God wants me to come to the place where I can decree things and speak them into existence. As a believer, I have the authority through Jesus Christ, and I have the scriptures to back me up. You and I can take authority over problems, difficulties, circumstances, and situations. I can decree that fear and confusion be gone from my life and those around me. This is part of my inheritance as a child of God.

Job 22:28 (KJV) said, "Thou shalt also decree a thing, and it shall be established unto thee:" Who is "Thou"? That is, you and I. "Thou shalt also decree a thing, and it shall be established unto thee." I can decree things when I know God's Word and talk in line with it. The devil has stopped me many times, and I am sure most of God's people from being bold enough to believe in the supernatural. We are limiting ourselves to what God can do by not standing steadfast upon his word. Once I learned to decree things and speak in line with the Word of God, then God take my word and honor it. If my words do not line up with the scripture, then it will not work. So whenever I speak in line with scripture, and believe what I say, it will come to pass, or has Pastor Joel Osteen said, "The word will find me."

In the previous chapter, I talked about the power of spoken words and how diligent we should be before we speak out every thought that comes to our mind. The spoken word is so powerful that Jesus in Mark 11:22–23 (NKJV) says, "So Jesus answered and said to them, 'Have faith in God. Truly I say to you, whoever says to this mountain, "Be taken up and cast into the sea," and does not doubt in his heart, but believes that what he says is going to happen, it will be granted to him." *Who is Jesus speaking to when he says "he"?* He is talking about "you" and "me."

The word is speaking to me, and I believe it. Read verse 23 again like this: "For verily Jesus saith unto me, that if I shall say unto this mountain, be thou removed, and be thou cast into the sea; and shall not doubt in my heart but shall believe that those things which I saith shall come to pass. I shall have whatsoever I saith." That is putting it personally to you and me. The mountain is (spiritual, physical, mental, or financial) "be thou removed into the sea and shall not doubt in his heart, he shall have whatsoever he saith." If the devil can keep me from coming forth with the boldness of speaking to the mountain, he will keep me running around all my life, wishing and hoping and never achieving that which is mine.

As a child of God, my life should be a testimony of God's grace and love in my life. The Word of God in Revelation 12:10 (NKJV) says the accuser of our brethren. That is us, goes before God day and night and accuses us. But in verse 11, the word says we overcome the devil by the Word of God and our testimony. That is why the devil works so hard to steal our testimony. When we speak God's Word and testify to the situations we face, we are bringing God into the presence of our situations.

Revelation 19:11–13 (NKJV) explains it so beautifully for us: "And I saw heaven opened, and behold a white horse; and he that sat upon him was called Faithful and True, and in righteousness he doth judge and make war. His eyes were as a flame of fire, and on his head were many crowns; and he had a name written, that no man knew, but he himself. And he was clothed with a vesture dipped in blood: and his name is called The Word of God."

This is awesome, the threatening of the written word he is going to execute on his enemies. The ensigns of his authority are his name, asserting his authority and power, warning the most powerful princes to submit, or they must fall before him. So no matter what the circumstance, I cannot be defeated; I am a winner. Because of the blood and the Word of God I can decree a thing, command my day, refuse sickness, refuse poverty, and it must come to pass. It is important for me to understand fully the power that comes when I submit to God.

As part of my morning prayer, I would command my day. I set things in motion based on what I put out in the universe, even if I do not see it immediately what I commend. If I do not stop speaking the words, it will manifest in my life. It was in this moment that I became more fully aware of the fact that God (our creator) wants me to experience everything that I wish to experience. Nothing can deny me, only that which I inherently deny myself. And while certain experiences do not always lead to pleasant outcomes, they do lead to a certain amount of enlightenment, especially as I return my thinking to the light and focusing on God's desires for me to learn a more loving way to live my life.

Let us see what God did. Genesis 1:3–31 NKJV is a good example. Genesis 1–3 says, "And God said, let there be light." What did he do? He said it. In the twenty-seventh verse, it says, "So God created man," and in the thirty-first verse, it says, "And God saw everything that he had made, and behold, it was very good. And the evening and the morning were the sixth day." How did God operate? How did he create and make? Create and make are two different words. Create means that he spoke it into being with his mouth. Making requires the use of visible ingredients. He made man out of dust. He took faith by the words of his mouth and created. He literally brought it into existence from an invisible substance called FAITH. You create something that is not there, but you make something out of something else. God needed to create, so he spoke. He said, "Let there be," "let there be," "let there be," "let there be." This is also what Jesus did. And throughout the Bible, we see that the prophets and men and women of God did the same thing.

We, too, are supposed to decree and receive. Give the Father's word to work in your circumstances, and he will do it in your life. But if you give the devil words to work with, he will do it in your life also. Give the Father, Jesus, and the Holy Spirit words that agree and line up with the Bible. Say what the Bible said, and all the powers of darkness and the devil in hell cannot keep God from bringing it to pass in your life. Confess this: "I say in the name of Jesus that Jesus bore my sicknesses and my infirmities. I will not bear them because Jesus already bore them. He redeemed me from sickness. I have health. He redeemed me from poverty. The blessings of the Lord have made me rich. I live in prosperity because Jesus said it, and I believe it."

Realize as I did that you are in Christ and Christ is in you. Jesus is the vine, and you are the branch, so if the sap comes out of the vine into the branch, it will produce the same things that the vine produces. The branch that is connected to a grape vine produces grapes, pears produce pears, and apples produce apples. The Bible says that Jesus is the vine, and we are the branches. We are in union with Jesus. We can, in this world, produce identical fruit that Jesus produced because he is in us to enable us to do it. That is how God will be glorified and people will come to know Jesus Christ by the life that is exhibit in us. We can go through life just using our natural abilities, but God wants us to learn how to come up into that spiritual arena, be seated in heavenly places in Christ Jesus, and utilize the attributes from our spiritual birth. Then we will walk in victory.

When God did not like things, he changed them. I did not like the way life was, so I fed myself on the Word of God and changed my situation. God did not like the void out there, so he said "world." He did not like the darkness, so he turned it to light. He did not like the bareness of the earth, so he said "trees." If you do not like the world that you are living in, get your faith working and change it. That is what God did, and that is exactly what I am doing. As Jesus is so am I.

Angels and Their Purposes

Each day is more excited for me then the last; I am finally learning to stop fighting life. By yielding to God, it allows me the freedom to be open to the universe that has been waiting to release what belongs to me. As long as I was fighting life and God, the soil of my life could not produce the fruit form the seed that was sown into it. Everything is now available to bring forth the manifestation of my destiny and my God-given gifts. The words I speak, the angels God assign to me, and the universe he blesses me with are for me to fulfill the highest expression of myself.

What Role Do My angels Play in the Manifestation of My Promise?

Psalm 91:11–12 (NKJV) says, "For He will give His angels charge of you, to guard you in all your ways. On their hands they will bear you up, lest you dash your foot against a stone." All angels were created as holy angels, but about a third of them rebelled against God and fell from their sinless position (Rev. 12:9, NKJV). Satan, the leader of the "bad" or fallen angels, is a liar, a murderer, and a thief (John 10:10, NKJV). He hates God, and he passionately hates God's people. We must always be aware of the two kinds of angelic activity in the world, good and evil. The scriptures tell us to try (i.e., test) the spirits to see if they are from God. Everything God created is different in some ways, even the angels.

In scriptures, it appears that angels are not confined to any specific form or shape but assume various forms and appearances according to the nature of the work they are required to perform and the will of God. In many instances, they behave and act just like we do. They sit, stand, look like women, look like men, talk, eat and sing. In other instances, the Bible describes them as being spirits, wind, and fire.

Angels have specific function and are actively involved in the lives of God's people. Most of the time, however, God's angels operate undercover and do not draw attention to themselves as they carry out the assignment given to them by God. I believe that although I may not immediately have known or see someone as an angel, they are there at God's direction. I have had experiences where a stranger has given me a valuable advice or assisted me in a dangerous situation only to later disappear. I also believe God loves me so much that he assigns me not one angel but five angels to see to my needs.

Why Do I Believe This?

The same night I had the vision of Jesus Christ on the cross, and I put my right fingers in his side, I woke up when I felt his blood on my fingers. However, when I fell asleep again, I was in the presence of five women. They were five women of color but different shades—two was lighter shade, and the other two where darker, and the other was in between. They just stood there smiling at me. I, of course, did not know who they were, so I thought they were evil spirits. I began to call on the name of Jesus. They did not move; they just stood their smiling. I kept repeating and repeating the name of Jesus, and nothing happened, so I thought to myself, "How come they are not moving, and I am calling on the name of Jesus?" I woke up from my dream puzzled.

So each morning as I fellowship with the Lord, I would ask him how those spirits did not leave when I called on the name of Jesus. On the fifth day of my fellowship with him, he told me, "They are not evil spirits. They are your angels." Five angels? I asked. I have five angels? You know I felt invincible after that. I believed nothing could touch me; I am well protected, and to this day, nothing has. I do want to make it clear that God does work through angels, and it is God who makes the decision to direct an angel to do his command, not an angel's decision to act independent from God.

Through this vision, I have come to understand that most of us have two or even five helpers. These angels mostly come in the form of guides. However, winged guardian angels (who come from the angelic realm) are never far away and always have a watchful eye on us to make sure nothing prevents us from accomplishing our divine purpose. And believe me when I tell you that nothing can stop them once they are headed toward a beacon of light that has just shot up into the heavens from a believer who is saying an earnest prayer!

What Does the Universe (Earth) Has for Us?

God gave me the vision of an international humanitarian organization over ten years ago. It is a huge vision, one that would eventually go across nations and change the lives of the people and places it encounters. Over the years, many people have joined our small team, wanting to believe they have captured the vision and wanting to be a part of it. However, as time went by and the vision appeared not to come to pass quickly enough for them, they would eventually, for one reason or another, exit the team. Not everyone leaves on their own accord. There were those that God basically put out. Their intention was not what it should be, and because God is always looking out for me and his own purpose, they had to go. The lessons are always for my benefit; I had to experience the different types of people who will and eventually come into my space.

And for someone whose hands are always open and willing to give of what I have, it was important that I learn that everyone who calls themselves friend is not a friend. The lessons were always painful, filled with disappointments, delays, and setbacks. The longer the vision take to develop, even though we had some success in different aspects of the vision, not seeing it come to completion on the timeframe I envisioned was at times discouraging. As the years passed by and the challenges became more enormous for both the organization and my own well-being seems to be threatened, my faith no longer seemed to or stand on the same foundation it did in the beginning of my journey when I thought nothing could stop me.

Some of us may have a dream or a goal we would like to see manifest before this life is over and actually have it happen, while some of us might have to wait to experience our dream in another life. No matter what, please know that when your desires or dreams are supposed to come to you, they will, and when they do, it will be completely fantastic! Until then, just realize that other lessons (that you need to experience for your own good) are being learned. And until you get what you want, my advice is that you are what I have adopted from Kevin R. Williams, author of *Nothing Better Than Death: Insights from 62 Profound Near-Death Experiences*, "Stop searching for or reminding yourself of the evidence of those 'things' that seem to be keeping you separated away from what you want. Whether you are facing a lack of money, love, good health, weight loss or personal success of any kind. Stop thinking negatively about these things, as all you will do is block the energy and flow of them coming to you!"[4]

Unfortunately, that is exactly what I did, released a lot of negative energy, which came back to me and block what I was trying to achieve. The truth is we all eventually manifest what we think about. We will manifest and find the opposition we fear if we keep looking for it! Because without even realizing it, we are subliminally building a case that will judge us unready to receive what we say we want because to the universe, instead of seeing an open hand to fill, it will only see a clenched fist!

Everything Vibrates

I grew up learning and knowing about the law of attraction, but this last year, I have spent much of my time learning about the law of vibration as it relates to me achieving my destiny. You will appreciate what you about to learn as I did, and eventually you will start to alter your life just by altering your thoughts and emotions. Unfortunately, many of us are programmed from childhood to have thoughts and emotions about worry, fear, and scarcity.

By changing these patterns of thoughts and feelings, however, we will be able to attract into our lives what we want. To understand this is to know that everything is energy. Science, through quantum physics, is showing us that everything in our universe is energy. When we go down on a subatomic level, we do not find matter but pure energy. The law of vibration is real. Just because you cannot see it does not mean it is untrue.

A popular example is the table; it may look solid and still, but within the table are millions and millions of subatomic particles "running around" and "popping" with energy. The table is pure energy and movement. Everything in this universe has its own vibrational frequency. However, we cannot see it, so it appears separate and solid to us.

Everything is vibrating at one speed or another, and so are we. According to Prof. John Hagelin, "We are all connected at the lowest level, person, animal, plant, and so on, a level he calls the unified field. However, our frequency is different from other things in the Universe hence it seems like we are separated from what we see around us, but we are not." As each of us possesses the spark of God within, or what Jesus spoke of as "the Kingdom that is within," we will all one day learn that we have access to unlimited amounts of power that exist on an enormous nuclear scale. This power begins as a seed or thought planted in the mind. If the thought is reinforced with additional thoughts of like kind, it will materialize and bloom.

Our spirit (or higher self) already knows this; it is just waiting for us to become conscious of this truth and see that we have the power to govern our lives by self-governing our minds.

Until then, the universe will deliver life lessons that must come to help us awaken our own consciousness, which over time bridges us over into divine truth.

Mike Dooley, the author of the best-selling book *Infinite Possibilities: The Art of Living Your Dreams*, is also the founder of "Notes from the Universe," which are short emails with humorous reminders of life's magic or divinity. In one of his notes, he talks about how we should think of our dream as they already happened, which is one of the key elements of law of attraction to send out the right vibration: "Just once a day, imagine the life you dream of. Believe that it can be yours in this world of magic and miracles. Choose to live, as you know of its inevitable manifestation. Do not compromise. Don't worry. Don't look for results. And as surely as spirit crafts one moment after another, so too will it fuse together the life you now lead with the life of your dream as if they were two pieces of a jigsaw puzzle, destine to become one."

The book of Ezekiel chapter 37 verses 1–14 (NKJV) is one of the great teachings that answers the staggering question we usually have about our situations. Can this dead career or this dead vision I have about my life come alive again? The Lord took Ezekiel in the spirit and sat him down in the midst of the valley, which was full of dry bones. The Lord had Ezekiel looked at the bones, then he asked Ezekiel, "Can these bones live?" Ezekiel gave the only appropriate answer: "O Lord God, you know" (37:3). Then the Lord said to Ezekiel, "Prophesy upon these bones, or speak the things to these dry bones you want to see change using my words." "Thus, saithe the Lord God unto these bone; Behold, I will cause breath to enter into you, and you shall live: And I will lay sinews upon you, and will bring up flesh upon you, and cover you with skin, and put breath in you, and you shall live; and you shall know that I am the Lord."

So Ezekiel prophesied as he was commanded. As he speaks to the bones, there was a noise and, behold, a shaking, and the bones came together, bone to bone. And when Ezekiel looked, the sinews and the flesh came up upon them, and the skin covered them, but there was no breath in them. Then the Lord said to Ezekiel, "Prophesy on to the wind, son of man, and say to the wind, thus saithe the Lord God; Come from the four winds, O breath, and breathe upon these slain, that they may live."

Ezekiel's prophesy as he was commanded, and the breath came upon the dry bones, and they lived and stood upon their feet, an exceedingly great army. Then the Lord explained to Ezekiel what it all meant. These bones are the whole house of Israel: "The people say, our bones are dried, and our hope is lost; we are cut off for our parts" (Ezek. 37:11, NKJV)."

Many lifetimes are necessary so that we might improve our soul's mental and emotional ability to create what we think of as our uniqueness as Ezekiel did, all so that we might come to know and stabilize our own intentions and realize how powerful they are! Once we realize how powerful our intentions are and understand that they do indeed manifest our destiny, we will find ourselves more and more able to access and incorporate any dream, wish, or concept we desire, as we continue to explore and evaluate ourselves in this lifetime. In other words, as we face how important our own thoughts are, the negative issues or hang-ups that might have blocked us before won't hold the same power, as we will have figured out how to remove the emotional and energetic attachments they once imposed.

As Kevin R. Williams states in *Nothing Better Than Death: Insights from 62 Profound Near-Death Experiences*,[4] "Not to worry, God did not send us here empty-handed! We have much guidance all around us in the supernatural realm and each of us have deep wisdoms implanted within our souls. They will speak to us in our time of need. When it is in God's plan for us to tap into this wisdom, there is nothing that can be done to stop the process! Just remember, God reaches everyone in a different way. No one person awakes to wisdom the same exact way. That is why God has given us such different personalities, life yearnings, comfort zones or expectations, as these drive us into the lives that ultimately rise us up to the inner truth that sleeps within us all." Through this process, we will become stronger gradually, and once our dream or request to God arrives, we will not only be able to hold or carry it, but we will be able to enjoy and thrive in it too!

Why Do So Many of Us Fail to Get What We Desire?

How many times have you prayed for things and they never manifested or decree a thing and it never came to pass? For me, too many times. Here is why. That is because our emotions and feelings are not aligned with what we desire. It is not enough for us to merely ask for something if we truly do not have emotions and feelings that are in harmony with what we ask for. We need to "believe" with what we want to be in the correct vibrational state. These are all thoughts, however. The true signal I am emitting is not a thought; it is a frequency. If we ask for more money through prayer, mediation, or just by wanting it, it will not help if our emotions and feelings are programmed to think that we do not deserve to be rich or that we cannot handle being rich.

Many of us grew up in families that if we ask for something, they told us money does not grow on trees. I heard that all the time growing up, and in return, I now say the same thing to my children. Understand this, our subconscious mind has a different belief system than what we are wishing for. Hence our inner feelings and emotions are not aligned with our desires. These beliefs are much stronger than our desires or wishes. So if we desire something like getting a new house, it will not happen if our belief is "I can't." The beliefs win every time.

We all have built a blueprint in our mind (subconscious) of what we regard as true and what we believe in. This blueprint has been sculpted for years through our childhood by our father, mother, friends, what we read in the newspaper, or what we see on the television. Then suddenly new information is presented to that blueprint; it will not automatically be added. We can ask for more money, financial wealth every day for years, and nothing will ever manifest as the law of attraction preaches because our subconscious is not aligned with that desire.

To gain the success we seek, it is essential to understand that we are not a physical being in a physical universe. We are an energetic/vibrational being in an energetic/vibrational universe. We are both a transmitter and a receiver of energy. One of our greatest challenges as a human being is learning how to live as a vibrational being in a vibrational universe. We do not attract into our lives what we want. We do not attract what we think about. We do not attract what we feel. Desires, thoughts, and feelings are all important, but these are more effects than causes. We attract what we are signaling. Think of yourself as a vibrational transmitter. We are constantly sending out signals that tell the universe who we are in this moment. The reason for that is because we do not really believe that God will do in us what we cannot do.

Those signals will either attract or repel other vibrational beings, events, and experiences. We will naturally attract that which is in harmony with our state of being, and we will repel that which is out of sync with our state. If our energetic self radiates wealth and abundance, our physical reality will reflect wealth and abundance for our physical being. If our energetic self radiates anger and frustration, our physical reality will reflect that as well. Since the signals we are sending out at any given moment tend to be fairly complex, our experience of physical reality will be equally complex. Once we can accept that our vibrational self attracts compatible patterns, it becomes clear that if we want to experience something different in our lives, we must somehow change the signals we are putting out.

I am learning from Steve Pavlina, author of *Personal Development for Smart People: The Conscious Pursuit of Personal Growth*, "that my vibrational being and my environment will tend to move toward equilibrium over time. If my current life situation appears stable, it is safe to say that I am maintaining equilibrium. For example, if I am financially broke, and if this is a stable situation that has persisted for some time, then it's likely that most of the energetic signals I am exposing myself to are also vibrating at a similar frequency of brokenness."

This includes the place I live, the people I interact with, my work environment, the events on my calendar, my furniture, and so on. My being is immersed in a field of these signals, and this encourages me to vibrate at the same level. If I continue to surround myself with signals that reinforce my current state, then that state will persist indefinitely. I may be able to get away from it for a while, but I will keep coming back to it if that is my equilibrium.[5] Not understanding what was going on with me, the longer I stay in this state, the more my faith was challenge. The more my faith was being challenge, the less I believe in the promises of God; naturally the negative energy signal increases what I was transmitting to the universe. And guess what I was receiving from the universe. Exactly what I was putting out, nothing but doubt and negativity.

Once I lost faith in God, things got crazier in my life. It causes my soul to lose faith because it is the inner spark or light within each of us that gives us eternal and physical life. To deny God is to deny my inner light, and to deny the inner light is to reject my life's true purpose and the inner power that gives me everything I am aspired to be. Once I lose faith in God, I will eventually fail to have faith in myself, which means I cannot perpetuate the higher vibration of self-love.

Inner love is the core power, which helps me create and maintain everything I enjoy about myself. Without self-love, I descend my consciousness to a lower vibration, and in so doing, I open myself up to lower energies, and destructive thoughts and habits soon follow that pull me away from my ability to tune into God, the higher heavens, and my spirit. If our soul does not feel connected to love or its own spirit, the human energy and flesh surrounding the soul (and mind) will begin to become depressed as very little life-giving light (from our inner spark) will have been created.

In time, if the behavior of faithlessness is not remedied, the soul will desire to leave the human vessel (and the mind it is attached to), and the human organism (aided by ego) will seek to find a way to die. Either a want for suicide will emerge, or disease or addiction (that will bring eventual destruction) will come about. And the human mind will accomplish its darkened intention. Thank God he loved me so much that he refused to leave me in that state. Writing this book was his way of getting me out.

How Can We Change This System?

When I am mediating in the quiet early morning with the Lord, in the absence of the cares of the world, the deeper my worship, the deeper my energy flows. I can sense some of the signals that are emanating from me. I can feel that I am radiating happiness, peace, and joy. I can sense that I am sending out signals to attract positive things into my life. I am sending out signal that I can accomplish anything I want. I can sense that I am radiating financial abundance and increase. If I am really in touch with myself, I can also tune into signals from my environment. Overall I can sense that the signals I am sending out and the signals coming from my environment are in sync. I feel happy, peaceful, and abundant, and my environment reflects that. My energy signature is the summation of all the signals I am sending out.

My thoughts and feelings are not the cause of these signals, though; my thoughts and feelings are actually effecting of the signals. Therefore, if I ever want to shift my thoughts and feelings, I must first change the signal I am emitting to the universe. Creating a temporary shift in my vibration is easy. You can create such a change in seconds. Jump around and move your body. Sing your favorite song, pray, smile for a minute. These will change your state. However, these will not create any sort of lasting change if you return to your old vibration afterward. If your dominant signal remains unchanged, your equilibrium will not shift.

Learning to shift my vibrational frequencies is so amazing for me; it explains so much for me the state of paralysis I was in. Do you remember earlier in the chapter I talked about having no doubt in God's power to heal? When I pray for some or myself for healing, it always manifests unless, of course, it was that person's time to move on to the next world. Because I had no doubt about God's powers to heal whosoever I prayed for, my vibration energy remains high, which allows me the powerful ability to see what is possible for me to achieve at my highest level. While my vibration remains up and in concurrence with my faith, massive amounts of positive and healing energy are created. But when it comes to trusting God with my finance, it took me a long time to release myself to the idea that God is far more capable than me to handle my finance. When I think of the many years of financial failures I had because of the negative vibration frequencies I transmitted to the universe, no wonder I struggle for so long.

During this state of being, my vibration gradually plummets, and I fall into a lower, inferior way of thinking. That positive light that allows me to vibrate positive energy to the universe becomes patchy with gray-like bits of supernatural matters now hovering over the place where there was once light. Because of this, the tone that was once produced by the light is now distressed and dysfunctional.

Here is how Steve Pavlina, author of *Personal Development for Smart People: The Conscious Pursuit of Personal Growth*, describes vibration of being broken and deep in debt: "a frequency I emitted for many years: tight, knotted, twisted, chaotic, rough, blurry, red, dark, fast, changing, pressed, and squeezed." Learning to sense and control the vibrational frequencies we are emitting is powerful stuff. Once we really get this, we can intentionally shift our frequency at will to experience what we desire. If we want to experience wealth, we can create that. If we want to experience a new relationship, we can create that too. If we want high energy and good health, we can create that as well. Steve is also correct when he said, "This isn't to say that it will be easy for you to accomplish all of these things. It takes practice to adjust your vibrational frequency correctly, so be patient with yourself. Rome wasn't manifested in a day." Below Steve shows us how we can shift our vibration and create what we desire:[5]

Shifting Your Vibration

In order to shift your equilibrium, you need to break the old equilibrium. This means you must create a lasting disconnect between your current vibration and the environmental vibrations that are compatible with it.

There are basically two ways to do this:

First, you can shift your own vibration long enough to create a lasting disconnect with your current environment. If you start transmitting a new signal, you will soon repel whatever in your environment is incompatible with your new signal. You will also begin attracting other people, events, and experiences that are compatible with your new signal. Hold the new vibration long enough, and you will see your whole physical reality change all around you. You can apply this approach by visualizing your goals very vividly for at least 20 minutes per day. Visualize in such a way that you can feel strong emotions. An emotional shift indicates that you are broadcasting a new signal. The longer you can hold this new vibration, the faster your reality will shift.

The second method is to intentionally replace many of your environmental signals with new ones. Then you must hold yourself in that new environment. This will feel uncomfortable at first because you will not initially be compatible with those new signals. You must allow them to recalibrate your own vibration until you become compatible with them. You can apply this approach by changing your environmental landscape physically, socially, and otherwise. For example, stop spending time with your lazy friends, give away your TV, and hang out every day with the most productive people you know. This will feel uncomfortable at first, but eventually you will start to integrate those new signals, and your own vibrational pattern will soon shift to come into resonance with these new people.

So, to sum up, you can either change the signal you are emitting, or you can change the signal soup you are immersed in. Either way can be effective at creating a lasting change in your vibrational pattern.

Creating What You Desire

To create what you want in your life, you must shift your vibrational pattern such that you are emitting a signal that's vibrationally compatible with your goals and desires.

You can identify that new vibration by vividly visualizing your goals until you feel different emotions, and those emotions stabilize at a certain point. Notice how your vibrational inner being feels, not just emotionally but energetically. Then return to your old state and notice the vibrational difference between the two states. Compare and contrast the old vibration with the new one. For example, here's how I'd describe the vibration of being broke and deep in debt, a frequency I emitted for many years: tight, knotted, twisted, chaotic, rough, blurry, red, dark, fast, changing, pressed and squeezed.

Here is how I would describe the vibration of financial abundance, open, free, clear, bluish-white, flowing, smooth, bright, focused, and intense. Each vibration has a different energy signature. If I temporarily shift my default vibration to a state of feeling broke (just by imagining it as real), I can feel my vibrational self-shifting its frequency too. If I held that vibration long enough, I would soon find that my physical reality followed suit. Hopefully, it is obvious by now that if you want to shift your vibration, it is a bad idea to consistently expose yourself to incompatible signals. Watch the TV news about the ongoing financial meltdown and the recession/ depression, and notice what happens to your vibration. Then notice what happens to your finances in the long run. If you want to experience financial abundance, this is a bad time to watch or read mainstream news. This is the perfect time to read high quality books, the Bible, or articles instead.

ENDNOTES:

1   Oswald Chambers, "The Authority of Truth," *My Utmost for His Highest* (Oswald Chambers Publications, 1992).

2   Linda Stover, "Casey's" critical thinking.

3   spritualgiftstest.com/spiritual-gift-prophecy

4   Kevin Williams, *Nothing Better Than Death: Insights from 62 Profound Near-Death Experiences* (Indiana: Xlibris, 2003).

5   Steve Pavlina, *Personal Development for Smart People: The Conscious Pursuit of Personal Growth* (California, 2009).

CHAPTER SEVENTEEN
THE CONCLUSION

A s I come to the completion of this book, I began to reflect on the statement that the Lord spoke to me a year ago when I was on this roller coaster with my faith and confidence in him. *"As long as we have been on this journey together, you still have not learned to trust me. Why don't you just walk away?"* That statement hit something deep inside. "What are you saying?" I thought. You are God, and you died for me. Now you are telling me to walk away. No way! I thought, I have invested too much in this relationship. I may have some doubts in certain areas of my life concerning what I believe God would do, but walking away, where would I ago? It never occurs to me.

That statement really began my process of taking a deeper look at my relationship with God on a broader and deeper way. I had to go deeper than my religion, culture, and traditions had led me thus far. This incredible journey, which I consider to be at the halfway point, has allowed me to discover a new world not a world that exists outside me but a world that exists inside me.

It is not that I did not believe in God; I just believed in my own idea of what God is. That belief comes with a fair amount of certainty, but I was often uncertain of what God was going to do next. These uncertainties in my experience with him developed into a critical and limited view of him. As a result, I also had a limited view of myself. Certainty is not the nature of a spiritual life, yet I believe I am a spiritual person. The journey of writing this book and the experiences he allowed me to go through were, for one reason, to answer the prayer of Jesus Christ. *"That they may be one just as we are one"* (John 17:22, NKJV).

I have learned that God is not concerned about making me happy right now, but he is continuously working out his ultimate perfection for me, which means for me to be certain of God, I had to be uncertain in all my ways, not knowing what tomorrow may bring. This is the supreme climb for me in God, and he could not purify my faith any other way than through the pain of tremendous ordeal. Whatever it takes God to break me from the traditional beliefs that misrepresent him, he was more than willing to do and did. With the right relationship with God, my life has the potential of being full of spontaneous, joyful uncertainty and expectancy. Jesus said, "Believe also in me" (John 14:1, NKJV), not believe certain things about me.

Once I understood God's purpose for me, my cynical and small-minded view began to diminish. To be God's disciple and to bring his purpose through me into the earth, I must make my relationship with him the dominant focus in my life and to be cautiously carefree about everything else in comparison to that. I was determined not to make the cares of the world that will confront me be the controlling factor of my life but to stay focused absolutely on the one that can see me through those problems. I must admit, this was the most difficult and yet critical disciplines of my Christian life, to allow the Holy Spirit to bring me into harmony with the teaching of Jesus on this subject. But once I got it, I realized the freedom and power that comes with this revelation.

I now understand that the greater purpose of my life could not be achieved until John 16:23 (NKJV) was fulfilled in my life: "In that day you will be one with the Father," and "in that day I will ask Him nothing." I will not need to ask because I will be certain that God will reveal things to me through the Holy Spirit in accordance with the will of God. This new attitude of my heart came about because my inner spiritual nature is willing to submit to the life of Jesus. As a result, my understanding has become perfectly clear, and now I have come to the place where there is no distance between the Lord and me because the Lord has made us one. Everything I mentioned in the previous chapters cannot be accomplished in my life until this happens.

Demonstrated by the Father's love for me, it is evident that my union with Jesus is complete and absolute. In that completeness, in the nature of Jesus Christ and my intimacy with him, whatever I ask the Father in his name (the name of Jesus) (John 16:23, NKJV), he will give it to me. This does not mean that my life will be free from external difficulties and uncertainties, but like Paul, those external challenges will not shake my internal being because like Jesus, I now know the Father's heart and mind toward me. This knowledge of the Lord is what gives and will also give you the peace and the untroubled relationship between God and us. In this space, I can no longer falsely accuse God of anything.

I am always asking questions like "What must I become to manifest the vision of what I have seen?" The difference today from six month ago is where I seek the answers. I now know never to look for the answers or the explanations in my mind but to look for the answers in my spirit. If I were going to live, or just survive, I had to bring my mind from the terror of my past and present life and live it with the mind of Christ. In other words, the spiritual principle of the Holy Spirit that teaches me must become spiritual practice in my life. By living on this level of consciousness, no experience, good or bad, can steal the goodness in my life.

God said to me if you will remain true to Me, I will lead you directly through every barrier and right into the inner chamber of the knowledge of me. This is what Paul means in Romans 8:37 (NKJV): "We are more than conquerors." Paul was not referring here to imaginary things but to things that are dangerously real. And he said we are victors during the midst of them, not because of our own ingenuity or because of our courage but because none of them affect our essential relationship with God in Jesus Christ. "Out of the wreck I rise" every time. Glory be to God!

"I Am That I Am"

It is now June 2018. It has taken me almost seven years to complete this book that has changed my life tremendously. It should have been completed six months ago, I thought. But so much has happened, and without these experiences, this book would be incomplete, and so would be my journey. As I meditated one morning, something profound occurred to me that put my entire life in perspective, and that is, I LOVE MY LIFE! This new discovery of love for my life had nothing to do with the false precepts I have been conditioned to believe all my life but who I have become.

Like many of you, I, too, once believed that my value and my well-being as a person had to do with something external of me. No wonder with this type of belief, man is never satisfied. The more we have, the more we want, never quite satisfied with ourselves. The powerful want more power, the wealthy seek more wealth, and the poor idealize those who have, selling their souls to have a little bit of what they think is glory, if only in their imaginations. And when that fails to satisfy the empty place in their souls that none of the above can fill, they continue to look for someone or something outside themselves to blame.

This vicious cycle will continue until we seek and connect to the one greater than ourselves. Now I know that every experience, good or bad, in my past was perfect because it has transformed me to what I am today. How have we as humanity lost what was always ours to know from the foundation of the earth? The knowledge of who we are.

One of the first things God did for humanity when he made us was to give us his own image and likeness. When the thought came to God in Genesis 1:26 (NKJV) to make man, he wanted us to have a sense of self of who we are in consideration of who he is. After all, we came out of him. So God gave us his great identity. But for us to walk and experience our true selves, we first must study and learn about the one from which we are made in his image and likeness. This explains why so many of us who live in our world are confused about who we are and are living lives based on false standards and beliefs of what have been sold to us by our environments, parents, and culture.

God, however, did not stop in Genesis about making us in his image. In Exodus 3:14, he explained to Moses what this image means. God said, "I Am That I Am that is my name forever and shall be known by this for future generation." I Am is the name of God, which is synonymous with us. That in the name means the desire to manifest in our lives, it represents what we are attracting in our lives. God defines the meaning of his name is not only in connection to his purpose but also to describe his nature and attributes and that he will become or do anything to accomplish his will.

The significance of this is that in the Bible, names have meanings. They say something about a person and, in a manner, define that person and his or her role, position, or destiny in life.

This name tells that God is beyond definition and comparison, and no limited name could be given to Him. God was making sure Moses knew and would tell his people that a being with no beginning, no end, no parentage, and no ethnicity sent him.

Self-image is how we perceive ourselves. It is several self impressions that have built up over time. What are your hopes and dreams? What do you think and feel? What have you done throughout your life, and what do you want to do? These self-images can be positive, giving a person confidence in his or her thoughts and actions, or negative, making a person doubtful of his or her capabilities and ideas. Your self-image can be quite different from how the world sees you.

It is time to create a new self-image, and bury the old life. Sever yourself from all the negativity once and for all, and create a new life of power, self-mastery, and accomplishments. Bring forth the infinite power within you that is seeking expression, that you have stifled and suppressed. Now call these powers into activity that they may find perfect and full expression in your body in the form of perfect health or a more fruitful and abundant life. Make this your daily confession and align with and become one with the infinite principle of good.

"I Am That I Am"

I am blessed in the city and blessed in the field.

I am a lender and not a borrower.

I am above and not beneath.

I will give birth to every promise God puts in my heart.

I am elevated to a level higher than I ever dreamed of.

I will overcome every obstacle, outlast every challenge,

and come through every difficulty.

I am in the right place at the right time.

I am meeting the right people, and the right breaks

are coming in my future. I will see every day as a gift from God.

I am exceedingly blessed and favored with prosperity,

healing, and success in my life. I am special, one of a kind.

I am God's masterpiece.

I have a sound mind filled with good thoughts.

I am full of compassion and kindness.

I am a breakthrough person.

I am calm and peaceful.

I am strong, healthier, and wiser.

I am the head and not the tail.

I am ready for a year of blessing and a year of thriving.

I am success, victory, and abundance.

This is my time to shine.

I am that I am.

In Jesus's name,

Amen.

Psalm 24
A Psalm of David

*The earth is the Lord's and the fullness thereof; the world, and they that dwell therein.
For He hath founded it upon the seas and established it upon the floods.*

Who shall ascend into the hill of the Lord? Or who shall stand in his holy place?

*He that hath clean hands, and a pure heart, who hath not lifted
up his soul unto vanity, nor sworn deceitfully.*

He shall receive the blessing from the Lord, and righteousness from the God of his salvation.

*This is the generation of them that seek him, that seek thy face, O Jacob. Selah. Lift up your
heads, O ye gates; and be ye lift up, ye everlasting doors; and the king of glory shall come in.*

Who is the King of glory? The Lord strong and mighty, the Lord mighty in battle.

*Lift up your heads, O ye gates; even lift them up, ye everlasting
doors; and the king of Glory shall come in.*

Who is this King of glory? The Lord of hosts, he is the King of glory. Selah

ABOUT THE AUTHOR

Maurine McFarlane is best known for writing supernatural and spiritual works. She is the author of *Releasing the Prophetic Destiny in Philadelphia: A City Under Reconstruction*, published in 2009. She does her best writing at the break of dawn, waking up from a transformational revelation from God. During those experiences, her soul has opened and received new insight of truth from the divine to give the word through the pages of her books.

The mother of two children, Crystal and Blake, she is also a humanitarian, activist, and mentor. Maurine was born on March 4 in Kingston, Jamaica, and now lives in Philadelphia, Pennsylvania. She has been featured in several publications such as *Black Pearls Magazine* and *The Philadelphia Tribune*. You can connect with Maurine on Facebook and Twitter.

Printed in the United States
by Baker & Taylor Publisher Services